# The Creation Of My Thoughts

*AuthorHouse™*
*1663 Liberty Drive*
*Bloomington, IN 47403*
*www.authorhouse.com*
*Phone: 1-800-839-8640*

*First published by AuthorHouse    11/18/2011*

*ISBN: 978-1-4567-3067-3 (sc)*
*ISBN: 978-1-4567-3069-7 (ebk)*

*Library of Congress Control Number: 2011907382*

*Printed in the United States of America*

# The Creation Of My Thoughts

James Duncan

# CONTENTS

The destiny and foundation of my Purpose is to obtain my father's grace.

Fully committed to his word and force that could never be trace.

With the connection to all spiritual needs to embrace the gifts of his deeds.

Standing high above the sky with uniqueness so purer and divine truly no one can perceive the beginning of time.

A true poet knows the definition of life and studies, and also the heart and mind.

Time is also on point within the sleep of his inner soul spirit.

The knowledge that God provides for him or her is to grasper the understanding of life.

The key is the mind and the spirit is of love and the heart is of treasure and the soul is the kingdom to heaven.

The instrument of my heart plays the orchestra of a tune of harmony from start.

The storms will come and go but many shall know that god is the life of each awakening show.

I write a lot it's like an addiction of my thoughts begin non-fictioning.

Truly He's Divine the most high that truly shine.

I elaborate the qualities and opportunities of the glorification of God words.

As a sanctuary of love and a desire of flames within the imperious burning through my soul like firer.

With beautiness of his gracefulness contemporary and divine forever. And through the healing and stripes of every human being around his creation.

The conquerors of this reality existence in the sight of God.

Knowing that He's the secluded one form this life he's, the kings of all kings.

His knowledge is being aware of wisdom and that is something that you accomplish through experiencing it.

And that is becoming absent to the unknown one which is God.

Beautiness is generating from within that is blind from sin.

That graspers the soul of life with truth to be told for becoming the bliss of love.

Tomorrow becomes a better day with no anger nor time that can't be trace.

You can only imagine it or try to come to understand or base your thoughts on dreams to become an existence of this reality.

The spirit Judgeth of all things for the foolishness and wise to confirm it.

As we fulfill the destiny of our lives of life, love and struggle.

The Lord will lend all his power to help us but we must learn to be patience and accept his gift.

The mind thinks that it's of the truth but the truth comes from every living human being heart.

We must act as we speak and also to teach each individual leading them to ascending.

True indeed concerning spiritual needs from the Lord.

Deep poetry is the deepness of your most profound inner intellectual thoughts.

The thoughts of being stillness from within the purity of my soul.

As I visualize within my thoughts the deepest depth of my father's foot step.

Now that I'm free to see I escape the enemy of the beast.

So that day will come to be the many of a ton.

Prolonging your image here in this dimension that we call life.

Building your foundation beyond this reality that we call earth.

Combining your soul with this universe when we let these earthly things dominate the superior of our true inner being.

It is self explanatory for the mind to accept his power.

His force is very powerful and complicated to deal with but very simple to those that come to know him.

Life is beautiful it provides all kinds of sources.

Form within your inner being dealing with each individual concept.

We always trying to challenging each other with the knowledge that god implied us with Black doesn't represent a thug or gangster black represent a meaning of freedom of respect and understanding of peace and being soul free.

When the soul of your spirit leaves from your body there's nothing left but flesh and without no soul spirit or mind how can your body function?

Because of the power of the manifestation from God, gives us faith and to do His will.

Everything as a human being is related to the seen and the unseen but we can't see this power.

But we as humans know that there's wisdom and supreme power in god's plan.

The mind creates a partial beautiful structure for enjoyment.

Its partition is of being of love filled with such excitement and very intelligent.

For the world to see it's dreams unfold unto the reality of existence.

The mind is always infuriated with the ego it could easily be mislead by good or bad.

For all human beings it's a struggle and challenge, that we must overcome that struggle and challenges of this world.

As we seek this world our minds become more and more adopt to the desires and material things of this world.

He's the master of this creation he made this world a tradition for all kind to enjoy life freely.

Time and space is built on a foundation of the secluded one.

Because without space or time how could the mind become to bring into existence of time.

So confuse totally mind abuse trying to beat up the self of yours.

When in reality all we have to do is to apply ourselves to god laws.

Looking into the four corners of the mind completing the distance between space and time of within the four corners of my time.

Living life as if it were a movie script because in the segment of each moment and second of each individual life I am that true being.

The mind of thoughts is stillness with peace and also it seeks knowledge.

The time of everything is action in whatever we do or become.

We must have full confidence or believe without no distraction.

Because distraction will destroy your true being all which that you believe in.

You must be able to express the trueness of your well being because we all live behind costumes.

The lord has made away for me he has been my comforter through my strife and dignity.

Love is beautiful it overcomes all of your trials and tribulation.

It so purer and sweet it has no meaning it is the greatest gift that the lord offer us.

But how can we live in peace when there's always grief.

The rich keep getting rich while the poor is suffering looking for hope.

I write what I see and feel my love from within my dreams become real.

My heart within my desire, my pain turns real so strong that only God can feel.

The blood of my stripes pertaining to each word that I write.

Sustaining these days and times wishing that I could turn back the hand of mines.

I guess if I was dead without going through life dreadful and scared.

I am destined to write the lord's truth instead your vision and dreams, and thoughts becomes the creation of this reality.

We as people don't have a clue about what the world is going to do.

Your eyes may get blurrier but try to think clearer.

It's just the thought of yours trying to take over your mind.

To recreate this existence to design mass wars and crimes.

For some people it's strange to regain their stability.

Becoming unwillingly not going insane you must remain peaceful and humble.

We as people speak out of justice when the law has been set for protection.

There is no unity only self contemplating direction.

So we as people must stay humble and obtain ourselves.

And keep the torch lit for the healing of our stripes, scares and wounds.

I got to live my life for the most high because he's my savior.

Without him my life is nothing toring down in the slumber.

All things that I go through will always be a struggle but with the lords help things will get better we just have to stay focus on the word.

Because when we step out into the world it's a viscious cycle out there that can't be untamed from sin.

It's so easy to be relieve from stress when you have the word in your life.

But we as human beings know that the dark is always near.

The four corners of your mind is to perform a destination of signs inside of the mind.

Your mind gives your thoughts life as it takes it stages through life.

We all go through obstacle hoping that we perceive from within to glorify our world.

The sooner will I try for a better day or will I not pay it no mind and astray.

Will I have a better hope for tomorrow or will I set aside my dreams and live in sorrow.

Will there be a purpose for my life full of challenges and strife.

Or shall I just give up on hope not defeating the purpose of my time.

Or shall I be the one lost crazy cripple and blind.

I became a king in my time because the Lord bless me with the great gift to design

To unite the highest of the highest to sing a song to glorify his throng.

I arose to be, He united me to see, the true love of His being the presence of His unseen.

With the firer in my soul being saluted with truth to be told.

Most nights I can't sleep because my dreams are so fascinating to me that I don't have a choice but to write.

I enjoy it my spirit becomes in tune with the Lord, my dreams get stronger and I begin to get deeper while the flesh is becoming weaker.

Beyond this reality I see hope but in this life, our life will always be pressure.

That will try to keep from ascending.

We never stop spending time taking the world creating it to be for mankind.

To me life is a struggle we cannot juggle it.

We face every daily day with a challenge so far beyond this cottage.

The end is near for those that are living in fear.

For the beast will tear your soul to pieces leaving behind no species.

These things I feel I cannot change these things that I see. I cannot nor do I fear man.

I'll always stand a thousand and one strong and yes my soul will transcend.

From the beginning to the end of time my heart would sound off like a lion roaring.

I'll boast the voice of mines like a trumpet. The present of my color will stand out.

Until I began to shout yes I'll make my life destine to the Lord.

No one will stop me nor will I allowed for the enemy to continue beating up on me I'll crush

The enemy with the tons of a million tongues.

I'll tap dance on his head with the crown of my throng.

Yes I will defeat the enemy throughout his purpose for being.

The Lords grace and mercy shall I follow through the days of my mercy and sufficient.

I need a little time to myself so that I can fulfill my wealth.

And inhale and exhale a little better out towards life.

But when I'm home in the zone just thinking of your beautiful smile just turns me on.

We can take it to the next level just as long as we take our time and not rush things.

Because our lives will go much smoother and divine.

Sometimes I ask myself why was I born into this existence.

Time is essence the purpose is of love because without love their wouldn't be life.

The creator fulfill his bliss around the elements of his creation.

I always try to feel the meekness of the word.

That quietness sound that tunes in with the spiritual rim of that stillness.

Those that conquers their obstacles on life events will be the strong holders of life.

Through praying consistently your faith will become much stronger and stronger.

The storms will come but as long as you believe in God He will deliver you from sin and evil.

His universe will be sustain by His grace to each individual that believe within His deliverance.

I know that the day is coming for each individual purpose to get to know the secluded one.

The world will be brought to their knees and peace shall overcome the creation of this life.

The reality of this existence shall He bring forth signs for the spirits to see.

For every heart shall be obtain to his word.

He will grant the best of peace for the elements for His children within this creation.

The beauty of your beautiness exsist from within the reality of the unseen.

That reflects off of the reality that Jesus Christ went through to save all his brothers and sisters so that when we sin or when it does come about us we know how to pray to Him in faith.

He has given us a vision to see His blessings fall upon us.

He will answer all prayers through our grace and by our faith.

We as many people suffer from lack of understanding and confidence.

Many things that we come across or deal with through obstacles or through life.

It becomes either a problem or situation that tears your soul down or by faith it will rebuild your character up.

As you keep praying your strength will become stronger and stronger.

The truth is through God there's no other way around it.

It is by faith we see eye to eye His miracles that He perform through us.

Becomes stronger within us by our faith shall we overcome our sin.

Our daily lives shall become much easier by faith and praying through your struggles.

Don't let the ship sail by you without getting abode it.

Don't let your blessing pass you by without receiving it.

Black don't represent gangster black represent a meaning of freedom respect and understanding of peace and being at peace soul free.

As I visionalize within my thoughts to the deepest depth of the Abbys of my father's footsteps.

To visionalize every designed significance thought that He has profound from within the hearts of every individual.

Deep poetry is a deepness of your inner seed performed within the inner dreams of focusing on outwards the reality of life.

True in deed concerning spiritual needs from my Lord praying that our soul is bless.

Act as you speak be real about what you teach.

Not pretending to be the one that would catch some ones.

Attention trying to perceive them leading them in the right way of ascending.

The mind gets the ego to think that's it is of the truth but the heart speaks out loud to the lord.

The fulfilling of this destiny that the world defines the definition of this reality.

The spirit judgeth all things for the foolish and the wise to confirm it.

Tomorrow confirm the attitude and anger time trace it try to understand your dreams for eternity.

Beautiness is from within born from sin that grasps the soul of you.

Knowledge is always being aware of your life and wisdom is something that's conform within the accomplishments through experiencing.

The knowledge of understanding and becoming closer and closer to the absent of the unknown.

The five star general the elements of life is power, a leader, and doer, listener, conquerer.

The cross is represented for what Jesus Christ died for all our sins.

The pymid is our middle eye which is called the knowledge of our ancestors.

The circle represent 360° a circle of God's creation of life and love.

For every star that god grants us with is an honor that means something.

The pain of my dreams swimming up the stream making the blood of my veins bleed.

Living day to day in this sin of flesh wishing that death didn't have no place for Eternal space.

Living hopeless knowing that in life you must stay focus.

Feeling your dignity alive believing in faith will set your mind a far high.

Sacrificing everything we ever lived for thru faith our dreams and mercy shall be restored.

I believe to achieve you got to climb the highest mountain and not to be afraid to try different things out of life if you mess up don't give up keep on trying that's how you achieve your blessings.

Become perfect no matter what mistake you make because one day you will be that winner.

And walking standing tall bright without no worries in your sight and make sure you pray each and every day and god would make a way.

This a lesson to be learn to all the beautiful kids from all over the world it doesn't matter about the color of your skin or who you represent as long as you are a friend.

Within god that's all that counts we all can be winners within ourselves as long as we just use our minds the right way and not the lines of the enemy.

# Non Fiction

The sounds of my emotion with the touch of devotion putting myself into the ways of mankind corruption being the inner superiority that we are playing with fire of hell balls

The way out of this world is within your inner self the life of reality controls the blind in every functional kind that lives in it the pretenders of symbolic back bitters cheaters trying to win this world of lost soul.

Stressing me with every thought across this reality hut hoping that I can capture my people from this dream I would like to face the minds of every kind that would be my blessing from God.

For me to pull the lost through this uncalled for bidden form of salvation. The sounds that control the self of being the full consists structure of god's art.

Being though god is the creator of love, that flows through resources material needs completing this earth with every two kind thing in the sight of love.

The philosophy that he is creating his time out of a book with a kindness mind full of joy spending and kindling for the price he paid for those to reap life everlasting joy.

Be hold the beholder of the lord, the almighty has come for the price of love covering the shield of breast amor with white stone over the beauty of his heart.

The angels are leading him to the race for the freedom of his children that are lost in the cross fire of blindness, he is a forgiver of life struggles and trials and tribulations when life seems tough for this beauty he's there to save you from your deadly curer.

So therefore as we say, life is no time to play for they must see the image of the secretive one when time has come for the lord to claim his structure of creation built upon his foundation of grace blessing his children from birth and putting them first on earth for the throne of grace with chemicals of dust into the soul of his unknown spreading the feeling of chromosome into the flesh to cover up the spirit. When for the reason of not to be exposed in this reality of the human being as now existence of this world. So to say as we live this reality day by day praying to our father for the wisdom to win this race.

A king I strive, the strings I tie, every time I apply my fleshly sins to this world.

The devil just keep on coming at me with terror.

So, I try to stay my distance astray I gets scarier.

Every time I take a look into the mirror my pain becomes clearer.

To reflect on the innocent with a deadly curer.

The devils rebel blood shedding vessels between good and evil amongst the concrete of Jesus.

Life is a planet that has to be nutured just like human beings.

Has to be nutured and animals plants.

Everything has to be loved for a change of breaking the cycle.

Of mass wars of destruction that people created for their own greed.

That are in higher places and that can make those selfish plains and useless human beings suffer for their greed and big dumb mistakes because they don't care and they been brane washed by their kind or seen or heard devilish things and stuff that they grew up around or saw all their lives and that cycle wasn't never broke so as they grew up.

They carried mass wars of greed and selfishness and committed they self and soul to the devils code for life as we are born into life god kissed us with his breath and gave us his gift of life twice we was born into a seed which was a circle of a three hundred sixty degree angle and then came a baby of his Eternal life to breed out of new forms of different life styles of birth.

So that we could live through his love until it's time for him to call us back home to be re born unto a life of love or a life of hell through the memories of our lives that we lived here on earth that god record why we was making plains to be called back home to be restored for our spirits to be hell bound or set free to explorer the life of love inside of gods house of gold.

God gives us these words for a meaning and purpose straight from the soul of the spirit each and every word that he gives is combine and conformed into his Lile form, life is consist of poetry everything around the rim of the earth is poetic love is of the greatest poetic feelings, that is so pro founded, only through god could just the greatness of that he has given us the soul giveth the spirit strength to believe by faith and to respect its most high and also to fight against the prince of palaties of evil doers.

Our life is constructure around Gods word just as we was conceive through our mother's womb we proceed the gifts of our blessing over night.

God harvest the seed of each thought over night. Each thought comes in time when we are at peace of laying down or just thinking and in the moment of each thought that is being birth it could either be good or bad but god gets the last decision in the end. So we live our life within our mother's womb inside of darkness for nine whole months and through those nine months god cleanses us and bathe us through unseen which we so call as life. Most of us make it the nine months of the, unseen and most of us don't it's our decision to fight or let go. Sometimes most of us just let go because we already experience other life forms through other life times before this one your deepest depth is found in the inner soul of your true existence. No one can confirm with god thoughts. They are unstop able and very unique and will break down any human or thing at any given time.

America we are living in the days of Amecedeon should the works of god decision be split into half. Just for this world to come to pass for his word should be done everlasting unto his son.

No one should have the second hand of time to tame none of his human beings.

We came to America her land that it would be peace amongst nation of blast that's why

Dr. Martin Luther King did the speech I have a dream because God instilled that beam within his heart and mind to stand up to her by the enemy amongst nations that the faith will be done into those that believe all people would hold hands together as one nation.

Conious awareness is what the ego lives off photographing life long memories replaying thoughts like an instrumental piano insured pride cut with the bitterness of the tongue mind to mind, seducing their own kind with fine pleasures for the eyes.

Blending time in many of the blind, the men's heart is misled, it is shred into tiny pieces he pretends not to feel the sharp pain shaking his body cutting through each fiber of life until it's too late his time is up he's doom.

My Book, the creation of my thoughts in which I wrote while incarcerated in the FEDERAL

PRISION SYSTEM. It is based on spirituality, politics and poetry. The spirituality part is because I was inspired by our creator to write this book. And because 1 believe that before we came into existence on this earth in this flesh. We were first spirits and once we moved past this stage in one eternal life. We will once again return to our original form as a spirit, whether it is eternal life or external domination. If we let our spirit guide us while in this stage we will progress in life. So many get caught up on the here and now, one impressing the next person, whether it be through material possessions or through our social status. Or through intimation.

A lot fail to tap into their spirit and living to please God. Living now and showing through actions that we desire eternal life. The politic part is, because of experiencing the pitfalls of our governing body. The trails of our people have went through in America. The things that we still go through today. A lot of things our people went through in the past still a affects us today, example the Willie Lynch letters written four hundred years ago were designed to teach the house slave to hate the field slaves. The light skinned blacks to hate the dark skinned blacks, the curly haired blacks to hate the straight haired blacks. The Willie Lynch letters still affect us today, that is why there is so much jealousy, hatred and killing in the black community. The melody poetry part is because of the flow of poetry. One thing about Art, Music, Poetry and Sculptures.

These are things that come from the soul, the spirit, and has a way of easing the pain. So the poetry while helping people to understand what we must do to accept in life. It also touches the spirit, so the desire to excel comes from within ones self. And not doing it to live to other expectations. The reason why this book should be of interest to people of all walks of life, because it gives outsiders and insiders a view of life.

# Chapter 1

# My Tragedies
# During My
# Incarceration

I was an inmate incarcerated in the Beckley Federal Prison in West Virginia in 1992. I have experienced a lot of crazy things on the outside and inside of prison. Federal prison is very scary. If you haven't been there, you certainly wouldn't want to go there, because prison is not fit for human beings. Believe it or not your life will be miserable, but if you have God in your life he will set you free. Most people don't realize being free is a joyful feeling. Just think about the families that have hurt because their loved ones are locked up for a long period of time. Just think about the beautiful children that have no parents to raise them because they are either locked or dead. I've been places where I have met beautiful people that didn't deserve to be in prison, and then I've met people that thought they were on top of the world, such as so-called gangsters, pimps, and so forth. I've met people that would put their own family members in prison, it didn't matter to them, and all that mattered, is that the individual that was locked up, got back out on the streets. It is said that you can't trust those that you think are all right, because most of the time those are the folks that you have to watch, and it is sad that people steal, and will go into your locker, and taking things without your permission. There were men sharing intimate relationships.

There were fights that took place quite often. I worked in the kitchen and the inmates were stealing items from the kitchen, and then sell the items for whatever they needed.

The inmates never got along with each other.

The environment in prison seemed strange to me. It felt like everyone was watching me, and they were out to get me for some odd reason. I was always the quiet type of person in prison. I guess that was the best way to be in that type of environment. When I was a young man, my father always told me that the wise will live long, so I took his advice, and that became a part of me as I grew older. Another reason that I didn't talk much was because you can't trust anyone in prison. Innocent people were getting hurt for no reason at all because of someone else's foolishness because of a person's pride. God takes care of everything when it's time, but the evil spirit is always near. I can remember times when I was just minding my business and the brothers would always be on joke time, trying to fight their pain away, and trying to run away from something they can't see, but can only feel when it takes place, not knowing the brother could have heard some bad news. You didn't know how that person might react, and a lot of stuff goes on in prison. Peace is the best realization that anyone could possibly have in this world.

During my incarceration, I was working in the kitchen and tragedy struck. On March 19, 1996, I was burned on my hand by chemicals used in the kitchen and water that was 158 degrees Fahrenheit. On March 20, 1996 a contractor came in to fix the machine that burned me. That same day I spoke with Dyal, the correctional officer on duty, he told me to speak with Officer Everson because the shift was about to change. I then spoke with Officer Everson about my injury and he sent me to the infirmary to see a Physician's Assistant and she applied ice and ointment to my injury, then bandaged my hand up. The nurse excused me from my work duties for the next day. The Water was very dangerous for the inmates and we didn't have support that we should have had from the staff.

I was taking dishes out of the dishwasher that belonged to the other kitchen staff, when I reached in the water it was coming through my plastic gloves and that is how my hand got burned.

I, James Duncan was an inmate at Beckley Federal Prison Camp in West Virginia. While performing my scheduled work assignment, I was a victim of a work-related injury once again.

On August 20, 1997 around 8:00 p.m. I was physically scarred and in ongoing pain. I was instructed by my supervisor Officer Donald Work to open a large gate that leads to the Powerhouse, which is a facility where the electrical, heating, and cooling systems for the prison. Responding to Officer Work's instructions, I exited the vehicle and opened the gate, after closing the gate I approached the truck to re-enter the cab of the vehicle. Another inmate, are Kennedy was in the cab of the truck. As I turned to approach the truck, the vehicle starting pulling off. I started to panic and considered the possibility of me being left standing alone, unsupervised near the entrance of the Powerhouse. To my Knowledge, an inmate is considered out of bounds if caught unattended in this area of the prison compound. I felt that Officer Work's supervision was unprofessional.

On the night that was injured, Officer Work displayed the same unprofessional characteristics as before. In a panic state, I chased the vehicle, struggling to enter the bed of the truck, Officer Work looked back at me, laughed and continued to accelerate, I then lost my footing and grip on the truck then tumbled to the ground, not knowing the extent of my injuries, I then jumped up chasing the vehicle once again, Officer Work eventually stopped and I reentered the vehicle, and Officer Work laughed as if the whole incident was a joke.

I started felling pain in my right arm then Officer Work noticed that my right arm was bleeding, he tried to make light of the whole situation, but he still showed very little concern about my injury. Once we got into the light I noticed how bloody I was, he tried to look for a first aid kit but I felt that my injuries needed more medical attention. Officer Work attempted to call the medical staff, there was no answer. A second call was made about twenty minutes later and we got through. Officer Work told the person on medical duty that an inmate hurt himself jumping from a table, losing his balance and scratched his hand, which was a lie. Officer Work suggested that I go along with his story that he told the medical staff person, he said if I didn't go along with the lie, he would deny the whole incident. By 11:00 p.m., I still had not received medical attention, by this time it is time to return Beckley and we left. Officer Work recommended that I go to bed and wait until morning to seek medical attention.

I protested the idea, insisting that there was no way I could sleep with my hand injured, bleeding, and unprotected. I followed Officer Work into the administrative building. Upon entering the correctional officer on duty noticed the injuries to my hand, insisted that Office Work contact the infirmary once again. The duty nurse saw the lacerations on my hand, and said "I didn't know that it was like this", she also stated that my injuries were so severe that she would have come to the Powerhouse. The nurse cleaned and dressed my hand and I returned to my housing unit.

The following Friday my hand was badly infected and I was in severe pain. A special investigator for the government was contacted by the name of Keith Schmidt and he documented the events that took place and took pictures of my Injuries. That was the last time I ever heard from Officer Work.

# Chapter 2

## Attitude

Attitude
A—Anger
T—Time
T—Trace
I—It
T—Try
U—Understand
D—Dreams
E—Eternity

The longer I live, the more I realize the impact of attitude on life. To me, attitude is more important than the past, education, money, circumstances, failures, success, and most definitely what other people think, say, or do.

It is more important than appearance, giftedness, or skill. Attitude will make or break a company, church, or a home.

The remarkable thing is we have a choice everyday regarding the attitude we will embrace for that day. We cannot change our past or change the people act in a certain way, and we cannot change the inevitable.

The only thing we can do is play on the one string we have, and that is our attitude. I am convinced that life is 10% of what happens to me and 90% of how I react to it. So it is within us, who we are to take charge of our attitudes.

# Chapter 3

# What a
# Woman
# Desires

A lady is a beautiful unique creature that I myself would treasure her heart to the fullest, walk the earth that my Lord created before the time of birth; they are the pleasure of the second eye in man's sight. So cool, that they can just about prove themselves in anything, and they are like angels in a picture frame. A lady has beautiful skin, pretty toes, and a baby face, what more could we ask for?

A lady is the backbone of our souls, created with love, the image of a baby so cuddly, creating hearts sweet as chocolate filled with love and heartaches. We as men come to find out how to take advantage of our sisters when there should not be one man playing the role of a clown.

The black beautifulness is an unanswered question, black beauty lives forever, its form is intelligent and the brass of its color is like polish that glows, never erases. It has a color of honor and truthfulness. It is always alive and strives to keep the flowing beautiness glowing. Every black sister has it. It is a gift from the father. No one can imagine the elements of black beauty pleasure. Black beauty is really structured to form the potentials of strength, honor and love for all power. Those are truthfulness of God's creation. All of my black beautiful intelligent sisters are so beautiful that I cannot even begin to even explain their desires and dark secrets of intimacy of a black beautiful African Queen. They are so much fun to be with and respectable sisters, their faces are like that of a Black Stallion. It is a divine portion that God provided them with and it is the beautiness. Nothing on this earth can take the place of the intelligence of a woman.

The woman's desires are like precious little symbols, full of so many unique things inside of her, that no one will ever see as a human being. They are beautiful images never seen before, not in your wildest dreams. Explaining my every thought towards some intimate one gives me the beautifulness to express my true inner feelings, so I must say there's so much in a beautiful lady that no one can take there remarkable uniqueness that she has. To be for real, searching from within, trying to figure out their key of love, you will probably never find it, because it is a secret no man has never discovered, the key of love, it is so far within the heart of gold that the game has been played so many times before, so many of us just seem to fail over and over again. First you must get pass the emotion and then feelings and then try to move on in for the finish point, but don't slip and make a mistake, because if you do you will be another sucker who lost a chance at love instead of gold ladies charm punk.

A woman has the same personality as her mate, because they first came from the rib of man, and though that took effect, that is how they experience the same feelings as man. They take the images of us and play their innocent role and get away with it. They have this beautiful uniqueness flattering capacity that would catch their mate of love, and they have the most precious sensitive look, as an angle that god blessed them with, the beautiness of life that they inheritance will always live on because they are so strong and holders of our back bones, and we are their kings and servants to serve them with honor until death do us apart the strut of their boldness. I love all my beautiful sisters full of cream and caramel that's so juicy and romantically enhanced. There's so much beautiness within them that is so overwhelming within a brothers heart, and kindness from the start that every beautiful black sister has from within. I would like to cares you and squeeze you and hold you, and please you until You become my true and only divine. My mission is to sedlice You and give You my black pleasure of the night with honor and delight. Like the game of chess, your move is next chocolate love! I am your knight, your stallion, stressing my deepest inner being, that would guide your mind though the maze of this reality where there is only pleasure and intimacy of intimate desires and feelings of fulfilling the game of love an angel that God blessed them with, the beautiness of life that their inheritance will always live on because they are so strong and holders of our backbones, and we are their kings and servants to serve them with honor until death do us part.

The strut of their boldness. I love all my beautiful sisters full of cream and Carmel, so juicy and romantically enhanced. There is so much beautiness in them overwhelming within a brother's heart, and kindness from the start that every beautiful black sister has from start, I love them.

I would like to cares you and squeeze you and hold you, and please you until you become my true and only divine. My mission is to seduce you and give you my black pleasures of the night with honor and delight. Like the game of chess, your move is next chocolate love! I am your knight, your stallion, stressing my deepest inner being. That would guide your mind through the maze of reality where there is only pleasure and intimacy of intimate desires and feelings of fulfilling the game of love.

# Chapter 4

## Beauty

I believe beauty is the creation of everyone's unique soul, a spiritual fruit, so strong, that it can never be replaced by any worldly thing. The beauty of the mouth is so sweet expressing itself with positive words so intelligent, the mind has to be. To stay alive, so the mind would have to think first before speaking, because of the ego and in spite of the tongue if you are not careful the mouth can get you in trouble, that is what happens to a lot of people that does not know, those are the ones that would lose always, because of their ego, pride, and the image of something that does not fit their character.

I know that beauty represents the boldness in every sister's life, the uniqueness of every beautiful color that comes in all types of flavors, all my beautiful sisters have the look of a angel built like a stack house. The million faces of my beautiful sisters whole dreams of images in my heart, just thinking about them. All I know, at this time my Lord creates the beauty from within the heart of his children that sees him from within.

But out towards reality, love has no control over anything, not even human beings, it is so deep, it cuts like a two edged sword through the hearts of two innocent people. Love resists no pain inside the self, uncontrolled feelings of any individual guilt; love is so smooth and tender, if you use it the right way. The beauty was designed from above, filled with the foundation of faith and secure with the uniqueness of love, so free and pure that no one can stand its remarkable forcing curer filled with your answers of every life challenge. That is in the book of your father's creation full of the past, present, and future of everyone's challenge. The eyes of every human being play a beautiful role in each individual's life. If you past through the appearance of everybody's life styles you will see the true one of yourself and that represents love. The eye is like a contact of visual illusion, the eye brings, the mind in contact of creating things of this reality. The skill of nature's existence, God is beautiful because he created this earth with balance and equal unity, but people have this negative infuriated image to take on the world, but it doesn't work like that because God sees everything in the heart of human being. There's no way around the force of pureness beauty has seen.

From the beautiness of his source came out the fulfilling of his joy, long suffering, charity, and love. Let the beauty flow, from the grace of love, to the faithfulness of the heart that God created from, the start, let it flow to be with our father that gave us life to sing hymns, the songs that God put into us. I believe beautiness is the creation of everyone's unique soul that creates a beautiful fruit that is so strong that it cannot ever take the place of a worldly thing.

Black pearls of love from JD the prince of time. Black pearls, so sweet, better than chocolate honey covered nut wine. My black pearls are so very unique it shines like the beauties of a sapphire's charm; its desires are waiting to explore that special beautiful lady that has her mind set on JD's world. Black diamonds and pearls has a gift to share with its mate, to give her nothing but true love that the world can't offer and that's JD's black diamonds and pearls. Nothing but sweet love and romance of charms and hugs, I'll be the pretender of your illusion. The science chemistry of love potion with the fragrance of JD's elements of black pearls with the full package of love, devotion, and JD would like for you to explore his reality and yours won't be the same, I promise you that. Black pearls of love is waiting for that very beautiful special princess that is willing to submit her forever grace to me black diamonds and pearls mystery. The dreams of your memories awoke my soul just hearing the call of your beautiful voice made me feel the pleasure of me holding you and glittering our heart into the moon light together. For you my heart is yours because you first loved me baby. There's nothing I would give for you. You are the light of every dream that any person would love to have, more precious than a diamond rock. I say you are that beautiful special lady. When I go to sleep, I wake up in a co?? sweat just thinking about mine, I miss my love and beauty. So beautiful are pleasure of me holding you and glittering our heart into the moonlight together. For you, my heart is yours because you first loved me baby. There's nothing I would give for you. You are the light of every dream that any person would love to have, more precious than a diamond rock.

I say you are that beautiful special lady, when I go to sleep, I wake up in a cold sweat just thinking about mine, I miss you my love and beauty.

I visualize in my heart the beauty of sufficient peace that god gave me from within. My birth of existence I was always with God from the beginning of the creation of time. I submit my life and duty to my father's will each and every day of my life my God gives me. I'll always try and realize the deep trinity that my father has with me. I won't base my thoughts on manmade reality things because of my Lord! Consistency deeds that he has for me only a fool would not know. The presence of the Lord, for He's the greatest gift of all!

Beautiness is so fine and unique, clear, pure and sweet. The presence of fear, danger, and discrete in blackness of the night. The mystery forbidden that it seeks. It's the pleasure of love, but proclaims the sinful world of thugs, robbers, killers and demons of mobsters, sure "nuff" ruff rugging and shrugging off lifelong struggles". In the eye of every man is the death of life it weighs wealth or everlasting life. No one knows the cock of the crow nor the hour of the son of man, when he comes, it's the spirit that reigns over the foundation of the world.

The body is a shield for the transpiration to get around in, just for you to abide by the rules and play the part of this reality. As you know in this lifetime, there's a reason for everything, in this lifetime. This is not our home; it is only a place for wisdom and repetition and to respect and love and shares your beautiness with this creation. So beautiful are the special effects that it has of the Lord's creation because it develops a special kind of element that cannot be explained in many ways. The truthfulness of beauty is described as an angel filled with beautiful expression that is so strong, and pureness like the sound of lover formed into a symbol of a beautiful rose. The sound of love is sweet and pure because of peace.

The color of our skin is a prototype of beautifulness, there's no different race, we all are equal as people, but we just have misconception brainwash that internationalizes the lack of communication towards every color. Freedom is not represented as a color, freedom is a highly respected word, and freedom is of you, the speech of your thoughts, expressing your talent of love. There's no race mixture in the nature of freedom. It is the truthfulness of oneself, beautifulness, and meekness.

The beautiness from within, blind from sin that grasps the soul of two individuals that are in love with each other, becoming one bliss. My beautiful ladies of a queen full of sweetness that appears in every king's dream, with pleasure of intimacy to fulfill the presence of being, knowing that God is the beginning and the end of everyone's dream. The beauty is to be as it is, to come God, created in his beautifulness, to be as one, living for the love of peace, I know because I live for that truth of love that is filled with grace that flows from out of a fountain from up above. Each and every day it talks to me and tells me what is best for me, it's so pure that no one can steal it or take it for a ride because it lives in me, thanks to the lord; he is my life forever and ever. The mind is a beautiful structure of joy; its quality performs excitement for the world. It's a part of being that is very lovable because if it wasn't for the Lord there would not be a wonderful creation, filled with such intelligence of exclusive desires to give and share with the world through its challenges of lifetime struggles.

The beautifulness of life is so unique and uncontrolling that only nature takes it's course full of pleasures and unconditional love, even the leaves change on the trees and also the wind that blows from all directions, no one knows the truthfulness of this reality, earth passes this reality and it still remains beauty. My god will seek and search for the hidden beauties that his children have to share and offer them peace for their sake. My life is to be his for my sake; I live each day for his love and honor, representing his word of faith out to my fellow brothers and sisters.

The heart is a beautiful symbol of love, full of the creator's touch from up above, setting his signs up for the ones that truly need him the sick, blind and lost. Completing His creation, in so many fundamental ways of joy through this reality of sorrow over all, we are the history of this existence. We all are God's creation on the earth, breathing nature before we even became a name that was given at birth. We are the heroes of our forefathers that left us with dignity, believing in the father who created them with honor and strength.

The sound of your thoughts are so beautiful with no distraction flowing through the soul of yours with no form, but breathing what comes out this reality, giving itself action upon responsibility to either be blessed, or to either hurt someone. It's your word that makes you and God the one that breed the forms of your action. Full of participating and submitting your inner self for guidance from the lord. The beauty was designs from above filled with the foundation of faith and secure with the uniqueness of love, so free and pure, that no one can stand it's remarkable forcing curer filled with your answers of every life challenge, that is in the book of your father's creation full of the past, present, and future of everyone's challenge

# Chapter 5

## Feelings

My love connects the vibe of those that can feel the hurt that I am going through as a human being. The spirit of man has the will power over the flesh to acknowledge the self of one's hurting soul. My time here on earth is very limited, I don't know when my calling will come, but before I leave, if my precious lord is willing, I would like to leave a legacy behind for my family and my brothers and sisters. The heart of time is at hand, I got to get myself together because time is precious in this reality, a second of your time can make you or break you. I can't figure out this life's role of mines, and my family that I think about all the time. The trials and tribulations that we go through and what I think about at that point of time in my life.

Deep down inside, no one knows how I feel, there's so much stuff I hide by the wayside. The feeling of emptiness upon this dark shadowed space between the sky and the earth, calling upon my father's new beginning of birth, so I say the waves of the ocean are like the thoughts of a billion questions, so deep into the mind that there's no one on earth who can truly perceive the beginning of time. Looking from a distance out toward reality, seeking to understand, hoping to find out why we were put here on earth, and not knowing that we were already here before birth.

I think from the heart, not the mind, because there's so much controversy and negative child's play. So I say the heart of your time is your life and your words that you are, but little do you know, God's purpose is in you, playing your role good or bad, happy or sad. That is who he is, the most creative of all, omnipresent, that's what I say. The love of creation accompanied with faith, there's going to be temptation in life for God's children. No matter how hard times get, always look towards God for your loving shining remarkable set. Come together and learn the instrument of love and sweetness of everybody, cure the sound of your heart filled with so many contacts of emotional input feelings that can never be described as reality's outlook.

Just like chocolate, so good building your trust upon something that's no good, but avoiding everyday of your life from birth to believe that everything was put here first. As we see this world not as it is, but as a game for material needs and sacrifice to please our selfish deeds, to think we are all that, but deep down we are nothing, trying to use the next man with your own words, I guess we sin so many ways, we all try to be big shots by showing off over nothing, trying to use yourself as recreated, but it won't never work because it's your heart that counts for every moment of your life. Don't do it because you think you are going to get a break now, you might, but that will be a very hard decision because only the lord can for fill your pain, joys, and needs.

The sounds of my emotion with the touch of devotion, putting myself into the corruptive ways of mankind, being the inner superior that we are playing with fire of hell balls. The way out of this world is within your inner self. The lack of reality controls the blind in every functional kind that lives in it. The pretenders of symbolic back biters and cheaters are trying to win this world of lost souls. Stressing my every thought across this reality hut, hoping that I can capture my people from this dream. I would like to face the minds of every kind that would be my blessing from God! For me, I am trying to pull the lost souls through this forbidden form of salvation.

At this time in each individual life, they are dealing with a form of evil that doesn't make sense, but in the eyes of human beings, it is a game to them, they strive off of evil and cursing people for the life of living, just to keep currently coming in, that's how so many of us live in these days in times for self and wealth, instead of increasing hope and love of a beautiful generation of joy, because it's out there for everyone to enjoy, not to kill, steal and destroy. I guess that's how most of us live in this reality want it to be set up for I know within myself, we will always stay in form of health and strong holders of the earthly soldiers.

The sounds that control the self of being the full consist structure of God's art. Although God is the creator of love that flows through resources of material needs, completing this earth with every kind and thing in sight of love. The philosophy that he is creating time out of a book with a mind full of kindness and joy, spending and kindling for the price he paid for those to reap life's everlasting joy. Behold the bold of the Lord, the almighty has come for the price of love, covering the shield of breast of armor with white stone over the beauty of the heart. The angels are leading him in the race for the freedom of his children that are lost in the crossfire of blindness. He is a forgiver of life's struggles, trials and tribulations.

When life seems tough for his beauty, he's there to save you from your deadly curer. So therefore as we say, life is no time to play for they must see the image of the secretive one when time has come for the lord to claim his structure of creation build upon his foundation of grace, blessing his children through grace and putting them first on earth for the throne of grace with the chemicals of dust into the soul of his unknown spreading of the feeling chromosomes into the flesh to cover up the spirit when for the reason of not to be exposed in this reality of the human being now in existence of this world, so to say, we live this reality, day by day, praying to our father for the wisdom to win this race.

Me, myself, I don't understand that, he created this nation of reality as one to be the salvation of tons. the mind is a tool to create positive thoughts, and the tongue speaks of wisdom and knowledge, and the heart is of beauty of your foundation and it holds the courage of love.

All humanoids are blind and deceitful at birth, because of the flesh that blinds us from the reality of God's creation. We are unacceptable in the presence of God, but because of the spirit, he awarded us with, we might be saved through him of not being condemned. Everyone has their thought either good or bad, but so many beautiful people prefer the bad side of life, because as it is written Satan was cast out of heaven down into earth to take over, and that's where we come in at for being created, because without nothing, how can Satan control the universe, so God created people in his image of understanding, but his thoughts are higher than our thoughts are.

I feel there's someone inside of me, beside myself generating emotional thoughts from within forming a bliss of deep confidential information erupting volcanoes when necessary, combining beautiful melodies in contact with the inner meeting, sweetness and vibrations of spiritual reality, giving your all, as one building, your faith is on the promised land forever. Twenty contacts he provides, never cheating, always alive, forgiving easily, he's the almighty of the battle.

The mind is made of a trillion of thoughts that there is no process, earthly, limited desire; it would not select to provide speeding through the galaxy like a shooting star. The man who didn't love himself for someone else so confused, mind abused, intruders from another world trying to steal the blessing of God's spirit, the pureness cruising the straight road of paradise with a mind filled with false conceptions and wicked advice, conscious awareness is what the ego lives off photographing lifelong memories, replaying thoughts like an instrumental piano, injured pride cut with the bitterness of the tongue, mind to mind, seducing their own kind with fine pleasures for the eyes blending in time in many ways of the blind. The man is misled; it is shredded into tiny pieces. He pretends not to feel the sharp pain, shaking his body, cutting through each fiber of life until it is too late, his time is up, he is doomed!

The blackness and darkness of everyone's look with a shade that blinds the kindness of a person's innocent look. The planet is coming to its end real soon. The final chapters of the book are getting closer to the permanent doom! That is why so many humans are expressing their truthfulness of love, because they know! Life is like a lift off. It always has its excitement, either up or down. The earth of life is like corners of the mind as God created, the reality of this time, our minds create things and objects, while our father creates from faith. He provides everything in his time; he is the awesome one of every act and play. There is no one that could be the actor that he is, I don't think so!

He's the motion picture we are now watching, the earth that he created without a sound, he's all that! No one can defeat his purpose, because he's the time stopper of history, he's the game of each saying, he makes the call of everyone's awakening, the presence of his blessings are the gifts of life, and the big beautiful bright stars and the moon! Black men as soldiers are full of boldness and dignity. We are our worst enemy, full of hate and envy. The black man is always killing his own kind, when God designed this world for us to love one another, not to kill, steal, and destroy our own kind. When will the black soldier wake up and realize that we are only one, just manifesting the gift that god gave us. We all bleed the same blood and all go back to dust. When will the jealousy stop? How long does it have to take before God comes back for his children? The days of this life is coming closer and closer before time is doomed! We as people need to come together and learn how to love one another, because God is coming back for his children to be with him to join him in eternity.

I know the life of time is now for every kind to get themselves together before the Lord returns. With his book of life for those that are accepted in his paradise of love, born in the heart of doves with beautifulness of unicorns, with the pleasure of his heavenly sky tops filled with gold trimmings around his house, for those that don't know him, his kingdom is not of this reality. He's the king of kings, his beauty is unconditional flowing. There is so much he has to offer for his ride. He is the father of life!

He is the life of all of the living that has breath, for those that don't know him. I believe in my heart without a doubt my love is in his heart to stay forever to live life in destiny through reality for the strong and rough regrets. All names are written in his heart, and all faith is in the mind of his willingness of his creation. My God will bring his creation together as one union when the time comes for every human to submit their lives, there's nothing on this earth that can stop him for performing the truth!

I feel the man of God's plan is coming real soon to save this forbidden world. The souls of the earth will reap their father's plan until the shape of every human that has breath here on earth. The battle of the minds won't stop, but the changing of times will continue performing itself through the thoughts of visualizing reality. The mind must be focusing on these simple things first instead of trying to focus on the true Godly inner beam. The cosmic of glowing prospering like a fascinating shooting star. I know through time things will become clearer and more real in the minds of those that are fools to this reality material stage. The mind of a human structure through the fruit of God, just as grass grows; we accomplish and reap the heavenly gifts of the soul. The talent that the lord gave is always with us until the end. The plans that we have as a man is very unique, because of the mind, the gift from the lord that could never be broken down. As the days travel through time there is always someone doing something that doesn't concern their true identity. We are the source of every creating machine, we walk the land of suffering, being brutalized and utilized for our own kind. As I said the world is set up to be the beast profound. In the time of the beginning, when we first took reality into position, the forces clearly spreading like an epidemic of unsolved mysteries. The words of life represent our truthfulness to come in tune with unseen beauty, and not being invaded by the beast fearlessly.

The mind speaks through my heart with every bit of love; folding—down the significance of my love towards my salvation of innocent people, that God created with the taste of love, and not one he hates because he is the portion of everyone curer. The talent that he provides to everyone as a gift filled with a lifetime insurance record. The book is in the heart of every human being, that has the key of heaven that will increase your limit to higher things, and the way of this life, is if you let it, it will suck you in, and then it will steal your joy. For it is the sound and sign of the devil's code, full of rags and riches for the beautiful soul.

He is a thief living in the sight of human, and all he wants is victory over you, not the world, it is you he wants, and that's how he acknowledge himself through a loving a bitter soul. I once was this way, living something that I wasn't, created to be, so my Lord spoke to me and kept me, because he knew that I was consistent to be someone very special.

The emptiness filled with so many unique thoughts that can't be expressed as beautiful desires of this world nor can it express its pureness with such boldness of pleasure filled with joyful pain, time, and treasure. Who knows where the time will set your compassionate heart, for there's only one who knows the time and pain you go through for filling your intimate secure desires full of heartaches, mass test of boastful desires completing the backbone with deceitful hell, lakes of fire burning so hot that you could never know you have met your only cruelness of desire. The ruler of the world is yourself, locked inside a little glimpse shell lost without hope beneath your shadow hut, still waiting to be heard of knowing that God is you fulfilling your task before the time of child birth. Like I said once before, we know this world as a game, not as a reality full of so many spiritual needs and desires that can be answered only if we seek this unique source of willingness, love, and fire.

The mind has a zillion of thoughts filled with beautiful things beyond this world, that your flesh could never desire a cut pearl, smooth as silk, but designed for knowledge and wisdom that would take you to a higher stage of college. So society has this depression of being the ruler of all, I must say man's biggest mistake is his downfall. We see things as if it was a Joke, but the clown gets the end of the slope. There's so much waiting down the line for the man with a plan, if there's no justice, who in the hell is going to select him I must say freedom has it's choices of opportunities. As the days become crueler, the wicked rulers take the world into their hands, filled with sinners beyond this ungraceful master devil's plans. The end is nearby for those who are ready, not the ones that are still killing and thinking that they are going to live forever, so I must say you will be waiting because your time is fading.

We were not put here on earth to be judged until they brought misconception unequal rights into this mentality, that's when the hold concept changed for equal rights reality. God has created his object of human beings to take the place of his stars that are up in heaven for his wonderful unique atmosphere of reality needs. God provides us the reality that no human has never seen before, but can only see the image of the thought. Seeking to be taught so many different things, trying to fit into my brain, into this world that is off limits for righteous ones, claiming something that's already begun, knowing that we already lost the fight, because God is the one we fear at sight: The world that the lord created before birth in so many ways that we turn it around, and use it for our territory, destroying each other by the tongue of the curse. Through your eyes I am what you are living for; to serve my people with the gift you've blessed me with. I know there are some lost souls out there that are feeling guilty about themselves for so many unpleasant reasons, but someone like me needs them as much as they need me, because they are a big inspiration to me for the help that they gave me, the encouragement, the inner self expressing myself all across this reality of existence. The time has come for a young brother by the name of James Daniel Duncan; yes that is me, my brothers and sisters.

Time is a substance from controlling the worldly nature of things changing the next person's mind on something he or she was supposed to do. Time is very difficult to relate to as humans because everything that is here was meant to already be the way that it is, because of our minds that God gave us from the beginning of time. We as men found a way to use it and harness those things that were already here and used it against our own kind, and that's how we became enemies towards one another, for things of this nature that God left here for us to share, not for us to be of greed and once we die, we leave our trails behind filled of bloody beasts and grief, but the only thing to remember is where I came from, and that's from nothing to become someone inside out. We came as family, an illusion, a name that my spirit represents me to be. Sometimes I see my brothers, the spirit, that I am how they look at each other out of envy. It's a crying shame, it hurts, me so much to see another one of God spirits of knowledge that the true father shines in our hearts each and every day. The simple things we think are so important to us are the things we die for, not even knowing that there's life after death everyday, that we wake up, we focus our life on making money in a positive or negative way. There's so much we need to make up for, I ask myself, how do I start this relationship from within? I try each and every day not to sin, but it's hard trying to beat yourself at your own superficial game of reality. The chances are very slim for a human. The word human comes from flesh and being comes from reality being at that state of peace, that is how human beings became to be sinful of the flesh and peace is of the spirit, the secluded one time is brilliant because nobody knows the day, they will die, I believe time is alive and it lives in the mind of every individual, I believe without time, we would be lost into this so called reality. The mind of creatures has a time limit on desires of the flesh because it's not pure.

In every man's heart, the darkness is always near, full of hatred and demons like the spark of the remarkable beasts tears, created something evil from within, not knowing how you all are blind with the devil's touch of every moment fear, searching to want more and more of that taste of evil's cure to every man's test is a game we play for keeps to learn the cubit of love fulfilling his inner peace so far deep no one has ever been, not knowing, searching for someone pure, stretching arms out for the love of yours, not to say seeking to be insecure now as the time slide by for every individual's visual playing the role of wanna be's, not knowing that you all are inner seeds developing from a higher creator so far beyond this earth that no one has ever seen his face before birth.

The dark age times are coming so fast, that no one has an idea about what to think, so many of us are lost in this fix with gun triggers of old time flicks, trying to relive a movie script fulfilling your game plan lick, not knowing you are another statistic trick, trying to get paid, looking to get laid making all types of moves to persuade yourself from staying in health, not knowing that God is the eyes of this world, watching you from your point of view. Shocking as it is, the beginning of your time doing everything unjustified, spitting out smart remarks without a doubt thinking you know everything, trying to criticize everyone worshipping idols for your soul. Blackness of every man, beauty is filled with so much unique talent so far beyond this fragile facility that will never be explained in humility ways of thinking with knowledge that would succeed your faith to a higher stage of college.

I ask myself, time and time again, what's wrong with me? I don't know, so I try to understand myself and my thoughts, I don't know at this time of my life, maybe I am confused of myself and thoughts, but it's so easy for me to fall short of the dec??y I know that the Lord is there for me. The times are hard, don't get me wrong, it's not easy, but nothing ever comes easy without a fight. I know that I am human and also temptation will catch up with me, but I keep telling myself that my God loves me, and also I live in the flesh, so I expect to sin, but to ask to be forgiven for that sin, the lord will forgive, because he loves us forever but he's not of this so called world, he can't accept us with sin, because when he first created us, he created us with love, and not sin that has no meaning with the creation of love.

There are so many unique people as Mr. Virgil, with his godliness, teaching so I must say I acknowledge people like him. The thoughts of my feelings don't equal up to responsibility of my manhood, because there is always some negative reaction, trying to pull me down, but we all know life is a struggle because without the pressure there would be nothing special. Stupidity is everyone's lack of concern, falling down from university understanding the mind level of conscious is where we seem to tolerate and settle better at fools of disguise mark of the devils between the eyes full of jealousy, no time to play to get your life straight because the sooner you are aware of the devils snakes is out to kill.

The directional road through life, those who cross the path of the easy way out without a fight, falls by the wayside filled with so many threats of sorrow and regrets. There are few that would only survive life exposure with so many blasphemers until there are only you. Treating thy self of yours exploring the glory of life, itself filled with so many unique words of knowledge despite all evil putting, it aside and focusing on my lord who high. Congratulating the self for not becoming someone else, who's letting the ego start every individual movie script, acting as if it were real, why the ego is steadily creating more problems of your life's movie script. Every time I have these dreams, like there's someone in living the script of my scene, so far and deep, where there's no one to turn to in reality appears, just blackness so confused and scared, seeking to find my way back, but there's no outdoor in the mind, trying so hard to fight this dream of my darkest illusion in time. The heartbeat is like a precious charm full of your life that controls secrets and valuable filled with so many rubies and gold, trimming around the cutlass part of your boutique ness, guarded by so many unique angels filled with so many loving kindness growth of unity realizing that skills is the meekness of the future. The more I learn about people, the less I understand and everyday this world we made gets a bit more out of hand; people desert their families and are cruel to their friends. The government spends our money planning wars that no one wins. Love is love and sex is sex. Whenever the two shall meet so many hearts are shattered before they really learn to beat. I've seen broken dreams and promises and the joys of true romance, the more I learn about people, the more I appreciate plants.

Everybody has a mission to do in the eyes of God, some fall off the path, many die without knowing, and most of us live on by seeking within the inner self and praying for help and comfort from the lord. The destiny of our lives are written in the book of revelations to be as it is the end of time, so to say splitting the souls up between heaven and hell. It's scary, but that's how life operates, it's a mystery. So I say to be a king we have to understand the knowledge that our fathers gave us through history.

Deep 'POETRY' is the inner grain of confounding intellectual thoughts proceeding towards reality of being conformed in so many ways, it has its foundation of being greater and defining it's meaning towards human beings. It doesn't take a fault in its word, because it's from the truth. I am your messiah, the king of my queen; I am supposed to serve with all my heart and gratitude. The thoughts of being as stillness is created from something that's pure, something that is so powerful that no one could never touch in this flesh and desire, we are the intimate ones of our true nature. Expressing our birth's talent in so many unique ways, finishing time in the eyes of materialistic deeds instead of putting time in for your lord constant needs, stressing your insecure time playing the role of the dumb, deaf, and blind. Struggling, killing, willing, trying to survive by making ends meet, thinking there's no hope for tomorrow, lost in this black dark shadow, confused and the mind is totally abused for no hope and power. Where's hope? I ask, I sit the end of my time? Will I be the one lost, crippled, and blind? I have the power to decide whether I want to live this dark shadow of death, I guess not because God has the light of wealth that this world can't offer.

The clouds of the air are filled with passionate care, to fulfill the world's atmosphere, through a lifetime of challenges of fears. The beauty that it provides for the universe's eyes, being above the reality, supplying a life time of charity. Clouds are full of joy with memories of human beings lifetime stories. It's a commitment we make that deepens in our life to become the final chapter of life's destruction. The clouds have its purpose for being brought into reality, godliness existing from the point of the top superior in the form of purity. The clouds of the air create images of pictures in the mind, and the sun makes the crops on the earth grow! There's nothing he won't hold back for all mankind, but we as humans try to live in grief, thinking that we can take this dirt with us, but life is like this when you pass away, you build enough of money for the family to take over where you left off, and then when they die, it's the same way throughout life's mystery. Life is reality like a sketch that was acted upon by the meaning of faith. Now this force is indescribable, but it gives us all the needs and pays us for all of our good deeds.

As we all know the mind is a creator from the creation of all of the mind which is brilliant of all of it's unique ideas, the mind can confuse you of your own thoughts, painless times your mind can bring you in contact with, I know because I am living these times and days in my life. The mind, feelings, and thoughts are like a weapon of survival to your full extent of life, not for harm, but for the freedom of you. Inside the mind of human beings you tape and visualize the thoughts of being. The thoughts of a human being come from a place of inner being that creates anything it focuses on, it lives off of words and definitions of emotional feelings. The mind translates the creation of being able to know those things that are of the world. The mind is a piece of artwork that the lord created for us with the heart to come in tune with the chemistry of his work. Why is it that everybody wants to know what is going on in your mind of words and thoughts? I tell myself, it's none of their business because they always have an opinion and try to answer your questions, it may be positive and it may not be positive, but only the lord knows, and most of the time you'll know what that person is already going to say, so therefore you let the bliss of love flow from a deeper inner space.

There is something more than this reality has to offer, I know because I see and feel the inner being directing me to a higher level of awareness. It is self explanatory for the mind to deal with the power it holds, it is to pure for anything to come near its force. Separating the bliss of love from the ego is a very unique feeling, it's so simple, but very complicated for human beings. Separating myself from the world, looking from a distance, helping me to keep my spirit in contact with my father's trail up above is the way to stay, by renewing your mind at all times for the sake of your forgiveness, being freely open, expressing your love towards your brothers and sisters are in the seal of your heart for the peace of bond, praying each and everyday, while the lord is changing the time of his, in front of your past, present, and future, it's beautiful for the ones that see the eyes of love for presence and force of love forever in the eyes of the human.

A heart needs a second chance when love makes it's vow, giving opportunity to sacrifice you to the lord, spoiling you with tremendous gifts for your good deeds, true to say to take responsibility of your needs, preparing yourself for the next lifetime for in the beginning, the world is of the lord, will always be continuously of true inner deep feelings that is in rooted the soul. Your visions, dreams and thoughts are who you are, that the creator made you from. The coming of the forceful, deep remorse through the enemy's eyes with deadly desired, cutting the hearts of split

decisions mocked. We live our lives through thoughts and dreams creating this structure of reality.

Time is everything, time can be the best of your life, time can be divine for the soul, time can be used in a positive way, time can put into a negative transformational way, time is the beginning and form and thought, time is high and pure with rich feeling, time is departed in everything, time is in control of reality, time is set in the eyes of the lord, time is beautiful and is meant to be, time is satisfaction to come together and unite our life with God for the beauty of his creation. Fulfilling the destiny that the creator laid down for you is a life long struggle. The Lord lend all of his power to help you do good deeds to better yourself.

The feeling of being is beautiful because of your character that stands for your talent; I am a man of free being. Someone that is expressing my thoughts out towards this so called reality that we humans live in, once you learn your natural ability of being at that state of awareness you will learn how to deal with anything in this life. There's no purpose of not accomplishing anything in this life. Blackness is like the darkest hour of the night, so rude and cruel until there's a disguise in everybody's sight, digging your spirit up before time sitting back and enjoying the pain, killing the one you love, yourself before you meet the very true best, pleasing the seekers, the ones your friends for a piece of thug, now that your life is in danger, lost in reality with strangers. The controversy of every black beautiful stallion full blooded and vicious visions that will seduce your inner being. A beautiful lady has many images of being that messiah of reality dramatizing her trueness of being here for putting herself on display.

I make my words come alive, bleed and breath the sounds of my thoughts, I even make them rain or tap dance on the people I come across. My words are like lighting that shakes the souls of all creation. The pen is like the gun and the ink is like the trigger, and I'll lose on anybody that comes my way with a lot of nonsense that doesn't make sense.

# Chapter 6

## Gifts That
## Come From
## God

Fulfilling the destiny that the creator laid down for me is life, love, and a struggle. The lord will lend you all of his power to help you, but you have to do good deeds to better yourself, try to control yourself, absence of the lord won't work because you have the heart, the ego, and the conscience to deal with things that come your way. You might lose direction, but the whole concept of your ability is your true responsibility, because you must shape your thoughts with the lord and put everything else behind you, your past and part of this so called reality. Let the force from the lord work for you, let this spiritual thing become your life in everything you do, live for it because in thee, you are the unseen test unknown to you, that is why, in this reality, that has all types of distracting things, which separate you from your gift, and your usefulness, you should know that it is for you to take full advantage! Have confidence and apply this knowledge from within and the key will open to your mind and heart so fast, it will scare you, but it's for the good of your love in life.

I came into the beautiful creation experiencing all of nature's reality. I ask myself, why me? Then I think if there was no me, there would be another person just like me, because of the self and unity for us to be called as one. * I always think of the times I was coming up, there was always beauty in my life that was based on fun, I guess that is why the lord said as you get older you must put away childish things. I don't know where life's next adventure will be for me, but I do know this much, my father is there for me. All of my life I have lived here on this earth and have been blessed. No one seems to really realize the meaning of being together as one. My life has really made me see me for who I really am, to see the real me within myself, it made me humble to all mankind with respect that my father blessed me with from the beginning of time. There's nothing new on earth that hasn't been here before.

Better Improvements t at t e eye can see that shouldn't be and the mind accept it being perfect indeed that would please and grieve. I didn't know the meaning of life until I put my heart and trust into my heavenly father's hand and he showed me the way of his life, now don't get me wrong, I still sin because I am human in the flesh, but I can tell you this much, my heart is with my father! I know this because he loves me. He loves all of his children, believe it, I know from experiencing it. Only love can free you from your flesh speak the truth, it's hard, but nothing comes easy without a doubt, that is why we were granted with faith to submit the will our heavenly father, so that it'll be just a little lighter for us to handle. Little do we know we are of the spirit with this sinful flesh, over the unique soul, self making, spiritual wealth, and inner seed with a beautiful dwelling in a heavenly being? There are dark spirits and there are spirits of light. We all were created for a purpose, to make our heavenly father happy for us.

Life has no set time, such as if it should produce its own foundation, and at birth unto God, who plans what we should be. It makes no noise, only living in itself as it is supposed to during this lifetime because of God. He is life to those that see it freely, that want to. share the beauty of your expression. That explains the simplicity based on your thoughts and nationality circumstances that we go through everyday in life. I can only speak for myself, because I feel the way you should be feeling at times, but that's all life is all about. Doesn't anything change how life operates, we have the choice to either accept it or not, it's our choice. I have found the trueness in me and it has made a big change in my life. I really see things from a different aspect concerning God. At one time I was of the world, blind to the truth, as if a CEAL had covered my heart and my eyes. The storms are always knocking at the door when so many of us are so unsure, lost in the wind of scattered seeds that the lord created as human needs, the creation of time is designed to perform it's pleasures filled with lifelong structure. Beauty is to be found in every creature that exist into reality, so to say God is the creator of everyone's most beautiful challenges, a lifetime of struggles, we go through life hoping to be understood, not knowing God has already prepared us for tests of a lifetime, appearance adored.

The storm in every human life never stops coming, because of Satan, trying to steal the soul of god unequalness abode. We all get negative thoughts, but no matter what God brings forth a positive thought to overcome the negative thought. The reason for expressing yourself is to be understood and to make sure everyone around you understands you. God is the protector and we are the actors, it's like a movie screenplay. God is a force of love that expresses it's energy through all his children, he builds salvation amongst salvation. He is everything a person could ever dream to be, because he is the dreamer of art in structure. The darkness of space beyond earth is just like space within every human being before birth. Think the circle of all God's creation is built in a 360 degree angle, the circle of his creation that reflects on everything.

I feel my life is being free from this reality period. This reality has been abused by blind people that live off of grief. We need not to be lead by materialistic things. That doesn't concern your spiritual needs, but that's what the Evil doer wants and he won't stop until he destroys all the good within. I know that we are searching for something, but without God, how can you find peace? There's nothing in this life that important without me giving thanks and praises to my lord and savior first, we all have something to be thankful for including life and health. We as human beings, the majority of us don't appreciate even living for now. How can we make it and not give up hope? There is a way and it will always be that way for those that will initiate the first move. Life is seen through every human that has breath.

The circle of all God's creation is built in a 360 degree angle that performs its cycle around the earth. The circle of his creation reflects on all human's needs, if you notice, in anything a circle is the hardest thing to form. When God created this reality, he created everything in a circle of his time. Even as human beings, we have a structure of being designed in the form of a circle. Everything that God does is out of love! There's no greater love than the lord's love, from up above, this universe structure. If everyone could see the truth of reality, the changes and challenges, they would see things different in all aspects, even the songs have emotion and outlooks on a lot of things in every human life today, because nothing is getting easy in this lifetime. The evil never dies, but the innocent lives through a lifetime. The endless times are here, I keep asking myself, is life supposed to be like this? Like I said, everyone is coming out with these albums that mean something for this reality trying to reach out to lost souls of life. Life has a face for God's creation and that represents the circle of his creation.

God prescribes us our medicine and we are the ones that turn away from our antidotes, shining his remarkable light in our hearts. Plenty of control supplies your inner soul with under siege demand making you feel the power of his, submitting plans down even more lasting obtaining grace. The force of being who you are, letting your mind create images upon images playing a character of something that came to your thought of ego, feeding it with all sorts of knowledge, to produce more where that came from stressing your conclusion, trying to recapture more of the rush, freedom of economic prepositional terms for all equal rights, searching from within, blending negative situations down to build your faith on solid ground of peace and harmony. This is what we are as humans, a star beyond this fragile life of ours also a strong holder, and is invisible for those that have eyes of this reality with flesh covering them, that is only a mask to take the place of the true one self.

God is life for everything that has life and unity. God provides all kind with his gift of faith that would never be traced. He is a form of his creation. God is a blessing to his creation. He created this life for all human beings to enjoy. The unseen, not to focus on materialistic things, but to realize that we are the unseen flesh of another reality. WE are the soil of the dust that was created and originated from dirt into clay and then came the flesh and formed human prey. The creature such as the beast, but with access to wisdom, technology that creates positive or negative wave lines of all kinds. God is symbol of love filled with grace such as beauty of trace beyond this reality of race with the stars and the moon, repeating around the atmosphere at a pace of peacefulness within human completeness. The chemistry is a liquid of form in which our body flesh and temperature where created from the creator first. The layers of skin appear in some type of soil with the flesh and liquid form and dust of our creator of appearance of living and when the skin dries up into the flesh, there we was as humans, created by the creator of love.

God is fascinating. He's the glory of beauty so sweet and unique and so pure, that the taste of his joy is everlasting cure he brings us out of the darkness of our nightmares with open arms of love. He's untouchable and flows through the system of every human being with the grace of love, so strong that no one can deny his purity. The sound of his voice is full of wisdom and knowledge that obtains his foundation of creation.

If this reality was yours, I would be your messiah of being, submitting my lifelong gift inner being to my beautiful queen. I would be your king that God created me to be, the soldier that I am, standing up for my lord with honor and sufficient needs and successful deeds. It wouldn't be any evil going on, only freedom and love of sufficient duty, deeds for our God. I know that strength comes from within the inner man and that comes from faith and believing in our God! In this lifetime, everybody wants to be rich, but don't even know the real significance of being rich. Everything comes from God, the beauty is of transform submitting yourself to God, he will lift you up and above all things and he will enrich your wealth. Through this life plan, but you must believe with all of your heart to bow down to the unseen one, secluded from flesh, but lives in the spirit of every human being. The lord is the creator of life that is formed into bliss of love! With pureness that can't be broken, with the beauty he gives out of his care for this creation of art. The lord is to be first in the life of every human being, because he's the door to everyone's freedom. He gives love and peace towards humanity. The lord said, focus on me, and I'll show you the way to the Promised Land. He will make your way easy and possible for salvation. Human beings financing there souls for the devil's code selling their hearts for some piece of mysterious speckles tiny dot that has no feeling, but gives pleasure for a second when you can have the bliss of love confronting you for a history of lifetime, giving you the joy and pleasure for your surrounding, blending and turning your pain around for joy after a lifetime. Humans will never learn the fullest joy of love until they try it, I mean really try it, the taste is unique and good, once you taste the pureness of it you will never be the same, I know because it's the truth. The name of the lord will live forever, but the games of the humans will fade into terror, cutting their souls up into little shreds of pieces until the howling of spirit bleeds out to the lord for the next episode of his contracting beating. The sounds are like something that creeps up on you, that it destroys your peace of thoughts; it tries to kill the innocent actions of your character being the evil of deadly curer. The sounds of thoughts and words are the people that create this image of sacred device, beuitializing their minds, trying to demand evil, when the next man just comes in and takes the life of yours. That is how it operates; you would never be that secluded one that you want to be, sorry only God controls that field of spiritual careers.

I now know that I am here for a meaningful purpose because, I was once nothing. Then . . . Poof . . . I came to be . . . flesh and blood, conscious flowed in with the breath of life. Awareness . . . Logic, perception, and feeling came to me; I began to learn . . . There is joy after this lifetime. There is more . . . It wasn't meant for us to come into this world, experience it, and then die after seeing the physical materialistic side. I am sorry if some people think this because it is his time to watch us enjoy living this so called I reality of life that he created for us. But there is more . . . Think . . . Imagine . . .

The spirit is of gold that so many unbelievable people would love to hold, spending your soul as money, getting tips, and thinking that's so funny, betraying themselves for someone less not knowing that there's only one self full of bliss providing every man constant needs, comparing dark with light won't work because positive and negative will not mix. There's no justice with a negative situation, but with a positive situation you have a better successful chance planning your faith in God's everlasting hand. We already living reality before birth, just playing the part to relieve our life on earth, seeking to be taught, so many things not knowing that the book of Genesis is our source of need.

God has made his eternal life a movie script just the way he has planned it to be, because it's the trueness of everyone's appearance, here and now. This is his show that we are performing, showing him we are in unity with him. He speaks through music to us and all types of other things. He's the omega, the divine and untouchable unique one, he has provided for all his children. He's the producer of freedom, he gets the last say so over the act, that we play, he's the recorder of our life with deeds and careless needs for every mistake we cause for one another, he has everything locked up in his heart of cuddle. Mediate and think, my son what is it you want son? There's so much that your beautiful heart desires, if only you've put your trust in me. Why isn't your trust in the one that created you? As you know, for I am concerned about your life, everything you do I watch over you, even when you are asleep, I'm there with open arms and true love. There's no one on this beautiful unique earth that I myself created is willing to take the time out to watch over you like I do. I am sorry son only, I am the only one that can take you and free your soul because I first created you through the beginning of time. The beginning of my thoughts is so strong, devoting in time from within a solid form building my inner self up to walk upon that solid ground. Inner seeding, my fantasy of dreams to be real, shooting the start of time into the minds, with the flash from realities of past times and mad times of corruptible thoughts designing yourself to visualize a criminal with no life support. When you here the echoes of the self telling you shouldn't commit theft of the truth of it's beauty and completeness in everything we do, has to end, but God never gives up, because he's the show of everything. They share in everything, all kinds of gods! The government even has their part in it. There's no escape in the game but to know that our father is in the midst of our lives. I live each and everyday on this earth to love, and to glorify my father!

People are destroying one another in their own blood and the Evil doers are distributing the utilities for our blood destruction. We are our own nightmares with the possession of guns and drugs in our lives in God's creation!

The sun is rising for the glory of God's creation, spreading the freshness across the earth, the inner seeding with the development of his creatures from the abundance, from a higher place, he brings rain drenching everything with the grace that has been sustained for the substance of his creation.

Oh thou son of mine, in many ways there is no limitations of your desires. Search and find the key that is within you, for it is the life in harmony that is good and rich for the soul. Look to me for glory, because I am of you, through you, and for you. If I am of there, who can be against you? For I hold your life in my hands. Everything is based on thought of stillness before we became created. We were at a still peace, it is just like an object, but we are not that thing. We are the sound waves of our thoughts, so unique and unimaginable that we can't be touches or expressed. Our thoughts are the life of every human being, so incredible that it can only be inspiring by God's grace. The beauty is to be as it is, to come as God created his beautifulness to be as one, living creature, and that's of love and beauty. I know, because I live for that truth of love, filled with a fountain that flows down from above. Each and everyday it talks to me, it's the best for me, so pure that no one can steal it or take it for a ride, because it lives in me, thanks to my lord, he's my cure. We were already of the spirit until the lord created us at birth with the touch of breath filled with so much of the self. Wisdom comes from within, filled with so much anointing of bliss with the pureness that would increase from a stage in the heart of yours that is so unique unto the beauty of love, expressing you through the test of love.

We are the lifelike pictures that our lord brought into existence, scanning our thoughts and memories of some lifetime ago. God gave us these tools of his earth's foundation for us to use for his structure of intimate art, not to abuse. He gave us pens, pencils, and beautiful voices to love to express our feelings, up above towards his pureness. The humans and animals are alike in some ways because God showed mercy on our grace to share the likeness of both the humans and the animals. We all share this earth as one to provide these earthly things that doesn't mean anything to God's creation. Those things we really need to prescribe for, we don't. So, we let these earthly things dominate our superior truthfulness to thy self. We have inner course sessions within ourselves that is a nature that responds with reality as an answer, filled with words of God's creation. The spirit of one inner being of songs and full of joy for the love and glory, striving to be a star of so many children of God, speeding like a light through the galaxy of space for a new beginning of time, searching for the lost souls of his children that's in this world, full of matchmakers and clowns. God is the maker of everything, for he is the revealing of all earth's creation to the goodness of the pure. He built this reality for love beyond this globe, his plan is set for the mountains above the beauty for those that succeed in the faith of love, and he pours his heart out for those that love him with sweetness and purity. Knowledge is being aware of and having the wisdom of something that you accomplish through experiencing knowledge and that's becoming closer to the absence of your presence of knowing God! The spirit is the judge of all things for the foolishness and the wise to confirm it."*

There is nothing in this lifetime that has the authority over you, only your mind is a free inner being that the lord supplied you with, to let you know he exists through out thoughts and hearts with love. He gave us wisdom the prayers of our hearts, it's the heart that holds the destiny, the key of our lives. My lord takes my hand, and walk with thee to the distant land, oh lord I love you! Oh, I want to please you, tame me oh lord! My lord takes my hand and walk with thee, to the distant land, oh lord I want to be with you! Oh, lord I really, really want to be with you! My lord takes my hand and walk with thee to the distant land! We all are playing the roles of wanna be's, when we are all self inner seeds, developing from a higher creator above, not knowing that we all must be judged from within, which comes out of the fruit of love, increasing from the lord, above changing the time in his place and beautiful arms up for his unique creation. Nothing wasn't meant to be without some kind of form or symbol. Everything was set in the mind of every human being's heart for a reason. God marked his children with a belief of significant signed in the heart of every living creature.

The color of the sky, filled with the beautiful road of divine, from within, it comes out like a shooting star glowing with the truthfulness of

God, spreading his songs and glory from old times, histories and stories full of testimonies, that is the life of everybody, filled with details and opinions of glory, telling the survival of your life's challenges and stories. The key is the mind, the spirit is love, and the heart is the treasure and the soul is the kingdom of heaven!

# Chapter 7

# My Life
# Experiences

There was a guy who gave me the key to my mind, to open my beliefs up. Divine, I was first without a thought seeking for help until this angel came down to me and gave me a time to get myself back in the line. The moment that I heard the angel, I knew right away it was a blessing for me here. I am without a doubt, fearless thinking that all I am is a failure and quitter, but my guardian angel is telling me this is the thought of your shadow, reducing your faith to something negative, give up the thought, my friend because I am only here with you for a minute. So listen to me and take what I am saying to you, it is very serious, for you must believe in yourself and have a foundation of trust and faith and strive for your beliefs and don't give up, if you make a mistake don't stop, keep going because its only temporary and it will destroy you, so let it go and keep fighting to be the best because only you can do it, only you!

You know he'll be watching you from above but that don't mean anything because he'll always protect your spirit from all evil, but if you need to make that decision for the good to become someone better and achieve your goals in this reality. You see, I can't be there for you because I am not of this world, you got to be the best you can and prescribe for the world as a gift about what he taught you, what you learned on your own, and when its time for you to come home, I'll be waiting and your father will too and the rest of your family. Stay strong and hang in there, you can do it, trust me I have faith in you from long distance, my friend, you must trust, have faith, and succeed, indulge your mind to become brilliant. I know you can do it, we are all rooting for you up in heaven, just put your heart into your father's hand, and he will perceive your journey for you, my friend, I will always stay in touch. I am with you for life, so there's nothing to worry about, good bye until next time, and my spirit in the flesh.

The certificates of life is to succeed and to be the best in everything and never give up on hope too soon, because there's always an open door for you, for the mind to grasp on to, the days of this life has its ways of progressing its activities. The motion that humans go through creates feelings, and nuclear wars amongst their own kind. The Blind never gets the full understanding of their life! Because of the weak and corrupt ones, destroys their own kind, blending the wants of material deeds in with the structure of God's things. No one feels the pain like the creator does, he's the maker of all, just like passing his fruit through the land! The time here on earth and in the next life will always be his, because he's the past and present of this existence, putting his portion of faith in all his kind, for here and now! The televisions of this reality are like material that likes to influence the minds of the children of God! The outer appearance of each character accepts the nature of reality as a seed when we all accept the spiritual needs that the lord has plans for his children! The sooner we come to understand ourselves, the better it will open the doors of the abyss of the mind! The black hole of emptiness, where's there is nothing but peace and understanding that creates good or bad, with the solution to all problems! The destiny of life is a mystery unseen from every human's dreams!

The space of my thoughts speak to me with clear in tune, its like being born free of the spirit, the realization of peace, the spirit of my soul gives me these powerful thoughts, its unstoppable. I myself couldn't stop it because it's my purpose for having this gift. I know it truly flows through me uncontrolled, and I am happy about the expressing my thoughts, being the truthfulness of this reality, scattered out my freedom to all kind most of the blind. My designs are from the mind that creates its fantasy of brainstorming this reality. The plans of my thoughts are very deep, that is was first discovered to seek, anywhere I am, I feel the presence of me playing the act of being or seen, the thoughts of your heart create destiny from the start, until you've created another path that destroyed your start, the motion of the mind creates the strive of time with the thoughts regulating the reality of this time functioning like the chemistry of the mind.

The mystery of the mind pretends to accept its awareness as a computer chip that is built to destroy the concept of time with this high technology, computerized it will be to compromise without thinking about the next move. Everything happens for a reason. From the life of existence nor can anything be added to it. Everything that goes on in movies is based upon true reality, and a lot of us don't even realize it. People destroying their physical appearance to become some fool that doesn't exist, but only in the eyes of sinners that will taste the pain of the flames, when their time comes, always remember, you can't take nothing with you.

What is wrong with the young people in today's society? Connecting themselves as one, decreasing our salvation of pieces of crumbs. Many individuals, not knowing that they are of one creator, are under this false conception of discretional reality of scum. The young, beautiful, pretty ladies are having children, not being above the stage, decreasing their knowledge to some Stone Age college. What is wrong with this reality? I ask myself, time and time again, we are robbing from ourselves, not knowing it's a life after death, you got to face it for yourself. Old people are struggling, trying to make this world a better place, I must say in these days and times, there are signs we must catch on to because our time is the creation in our minds. The circle around your life sometimes becomes a dramatic challenge for the most of us. We are lost in reality, not getting the correct knowledge. You must submit yourselves to become the force of peace. There's only one truth, and no one can change it because it lives as the bliss, reaching out from open awareness, that is all around this reality that first came from up above, searching for his lost souls. He gave his only begotten son of Mary, upon glory forever and ever, to make this life full of stormy days and a lifetime of stages of struggles to look towards him for good times and happiness forever.

Feel the rhythm of the heart. When will the minute of time stop? Why do I feel the hurt of sorrow so much? Where's this great beam of light at? I wish that I could see it and live it maybe I wouldn't have to experience this reality as it is. As I feel the rhythm of my heart, the second, the minute time never stops. I feel as if problems grow much stronger and the days become much closer to the death of each individual that can't see past the minute of time before their life stops. The life of everything brought into existence of the father's creation, fulfilled with everlasting love, so pure, it can't be cut with any satisfactory unlimited, materialistic things in space, beyond the world is black with no light that can grasp it's pureness of believing how fast your thoughts travel at that distance between space and now controlling the darkness of nothing performs thoughts and creation. Why is it that everybody is always worrying about other people's lives, in a loveable or negative jealous type of way? They base their thoughts on someone else's feelings, trying to figure out where their weak spots are, trying to destroy them by the thoughts and words that they perform, out of their mouths the tongues sets the mind up for either negative or positive transformation to free or punish you for creating the work that leads to a book of foolishness or positive thoughts.

Life is common to every individual it is meant to be for love and joy because we were created from birth and then when we past away and go back where we came from that is held against us, because the time, we are living this life, we are being recorded for our lifetime, past, present, and future, but to God, this life only stands for a meaning, living now, but to us it is a lifetime of negative and positive output to people in suspense. The sweetness of love, so smooth, performs in a touch of beauty, generating from the heart of doves so unique that nothing can come through the pureness of the shadow's touch as it flows through the system of many individuals gushing out like a fountain of real purity and rich feelings with the lord's blessings of peace on it's covering top.

Time is a struggle for each and every person. People are getting killed over materialistic things. I ask myself, where life is going to lead me. The world of God's creation is being destroyed day by day because of the Evil doers wickedness. They are the blameless, shameless, doubtful, wicked ones of this time, but we all must answer to the creator that created us from joy and love, to be his little Gods, so that he could express his love and feelings through us. I must say this doesn't last too long. because everything shall meet again and many of us will go to hell and many of us shall go to heaven. Mediate and think, my son what do you want son? There's so much of your beautiful heart that desires if only you put your trust in me. Why not trust the one that created you for I am your life, your everything that you do, even when you're asleep, I am watching over you with love. There is no one on this beautiful unique earth that I created. I am sorry son, but I am the only one that can take you for a ride through time because I was here first, through the beginning of time to take care of your deeds of cultivating the mind to selfish needs of foolishness, signs eliminating your talent to a piece of crumb for the ego that plays those games and tricks, never ending, non publishing flicks, holding your soul for sale until the next victim pays the price in he!!!

The directional road is the path of a positive street purer, it is your choice, no one forces you to take this route, and it's your life, being recorded, not by man, but the unseen ones that live for you and loves you. I know in my directional mind that man changes a lot of religion materials. The bible was tampered with and God doesn't like that a bit, he sees everything, so therefore we all have a price to pay. Everybody, judges, lawyers, prosecutors, and all type of human beings, they all have a price to pay, if not here on earth, then in the next life, there is no escape, sorry! Follow the followers, as in the dead leading the blind, trying to steal the creator, being in the reality of time, defiling the creators with material fines of man made filthiness, from rags to riches, building the mind up into images of foolishness. Deeds of mankind would never succeed in the eyes of the father's seed, nothing on the earth wants to break, this force of killing his breed, over all he sees the pain we go through, he watches us from dark doors, still we roam from the points of far seashores. Time of the blind will always continue on with the hope of our father putting us back into the history of his arms, with no worry or bother. I feel there's someone inside of me, besides myself, generating emotional thoughts from within, forming a bliss of deep confidential information, erupting volcanoes when necessary is in effect, combining beautiful melodies in contact with the inner meeting of sweetness, vibrations of spiritual reality, giving your all as one, building your faith on the promised land fore.

Time is alive for everything in this reality existence that brought into this reality of time by its remarkable hit, splitting 4 in half, made two of everything in time of our forefathers past. Life is an experience for everybody to understand and not for those who run games and scams. The essence of life is beautiful to express reality of love for you to seek and understand, and those unique full of things above your heart has its reality to fill of precious cutlass gold, trimming around the stone of you. Life sometimes is a storm for those who won't let up off the wound. Sometimes we often regret the past but looking ahead would keep us steadfast with the father above. Life is like a fountain from within, that flows with the knowledge of your life out toward reality, your ability depends on your faith as you succeed in your talent that your father blessed you with for his love. When your life begins, your dreams will never end. Everybody lives for a dream of wants, not for the inner spiritual needs. Not all people are like that, but the majority 0tthetuniverse accepts those things for the healing of the 6-1a4fn that is so confused with the color of green, that it will destroy their true being, filling themselves with false identities of the world, destroying their minds of the innocence in the honor of mankind. The solution is coming for the souls hope to free those that are lost in the manmade of hope. That love steals and kills for pleasure in time with God creating, to provide everything we live for hand to hand we turn around and kill for, letting our most valuable precious selves get the best of us, decreasing our knowledge to some puppet doll.

It's a scary sight to be left out with no type of information inside of the body and soul, because in order to succeed, you must have your self together with the one truthfulness and that's the secretive one, the unseen that never has been able to touch this force, but we do not know that it lives in everyone of us for our guidance and to increase our faith and also to uplift us when we are down, giving us that humble unique feeling of joy, spreading out from everywhere to meet his final shore's doors, opening the movie of our lives as we live this script for centuries, not knowing that we are only playing the part we had in our last lifetime, different from this reality. Life is futile and full of misleading concepts of controlling people that are in these big organizations of wicked times of this reality. There's nothing that no human being can't accomplish because of their intelligence that we were created with. We are blind to the things of this reality that would someday grow old, these are not our true paradigms of our true being, it's just a setup to steal our heavenly trace and utilize us with the ugliness of the evil to scare us, mistreat us, and frame us with their material and money deeds infuriating us with the fear and struggles of the human needs, corrupting and planning doubtful, seeds.

Times are changing so quick that we don't even realize how the devil gets us into tricks. So many of us are lost and trying to beat the system. When in reality, there's no short cut way out to win, brain shocking the mind through so much stuff, your thoughts are awakening either in heaven or hell. Every time you think about something, it's either good or bad, so as they say, we are our thoughts; we are actors of some play. Capacity is everyone's cure being absolutely clear, full of intelligence for the love of beauty, searching from within to find the purity, scandalizing, brainstorming yourself through some testing, trying to build your confidence on materialistic reality that doesn't exist longer than your life's similarity. Life is a projection that creates the mind to either, accept it or don't accept it. I believe the mind is a structure that allows God to appear into the concept of that person, visualizing the spirit of God's presence with or without the knowledge to communicate; we have our own option of the freedom of choice. The blind is so confused and abused in this life, man may try to change history to create their way of living and only the soul searchers see the truth of this reality, not the rudeness. Day by day we live by repeating history, so caught up in the blind, until there's no escape from our daily challenges life signs. This history is supposed to be an adventure through life, but people misuse and abuse it and turn it around until no one can enjoy their wonderful walking the grounds here on earth.

The unseen is the uneatable ones and the secluded one is the lord, the almighty, the healer for all wounds. The invisible sees and knows everything your life consists of, because the appearance is such a beautiful bliss. Nothing can separate you from it, only the secluded one can limit your days of reality. The heart of my time is deep and the minutes and seconds I put into reality a purpose that I must defeat for the lost love, brothers and sisters that are blind and asleep. Hopefully I'll create a connection of lives, so every human being will enjoy for my safe journey abode this reality now in this society of reality. I sit and ask myself, what does God have in store for men in the deepest of wealth? I don't know what it is, but I feel that fig tree of peace and harmony through love. My soul bares lifelong meekness that would never be exposed, only in the eyes where Godliness abode. My life is God, I can't do noting without my God's knowledge of his son, I sing with my heart to keep in mind that God is divine from start, he's the creator of all human reality. How people come to realize life is meant to be? We as people are driven by will. It's hard to fight something that is seen against the unseen, I know because we as human beings all try sometimes in our lives, but the mind is programmed to think that way from the materialistic things that was built for this reality. Life experience takes the place of God's creation, perimeter around his creatures are all part of his art, the width and length of the hearts. He set forth for his children design for the love of beauty and secluded everything in his time for a purpose, designating his arms around this earth for his kindling, his belief in every woman's and man's consistence plan. The life of one that the creator created of some more and more of it became his salvation full of an army to claim God's creation together; we are all his children forever. Now we race towards the mark of freedom land full of justice with an eye for an eye plan, so strong that no human can break the power of the lord's plan, traveling at the rate of the lord's speed no one not even a human can compete with the traveling of God's uniqueness in speed.

The culture of this reality is life itself based on the nature's foundation of unnecessary needs. The plantation of our salvation is in need of help from the lord, the one who gave his children to enjoy in. We are all children and the reason we are all his children is. because he lives for us. Theirs no reason for everything we live for without his purpose! I don't know where life will exhale, our souls through seasons, I do know this much, God is in control of this reality. I seek his presence through due seasons and for the time that

I still have here on earth. It's like a dream that really doesn't exist, but it's as real as possible, How far you'll allow the force of your mind to accept the energy of the world to eat it up, that's how real your world would be, it's only for you to see and actually realize the force of life itself, the world of cruelty. Life is like a flash before your eyes, trying to understand and grasp, the feeling being laid back in a form of day dream vision. It's like strange thoughts shooting through your mind like a camera, its flashing performance and brought into reality to take action and progress into the souls of man or woman concisely proceeding and producing from the force of love.

# Chapter 8

## Love

Love is the other half of a complete meaning your mate! Love is the beautifulness of completion with the uniqueness of interceding. Beauty is love and I see that in all my sisters, love is what I feel to be real. Nothing can escape the pleasure that it gives. My love, joy, good feelings, Love can make you or take you, and it can destroy you or build your foundation up within you. Love is just a portion of being from your heavenly father above! Love has been and always will destruct the hearts of every human being. From love everything that has breath was created to come into existence from my heavenly father's Mission, to do his will through faith that he has provided us with! Love is everywhere for those who recognize and understand it. Love was created for nothing less than the price and that's the understanding of our heavenly father's creation!

Shades of everyone's innocent book the blackness and darkness of everyone's look with a tense. that blinds the kindness of everyone's innocent all existence is coming to an end real soon. The final chapter of the book is getting closer to its doom! That's why so many humans are expressing their trueness Out of love, because they know! The real truth of love! Life is like a lift off! It always has excitement either up or down! Life is like a lift off! The earth of life is like the corners of the mind as in God created the reality of this time our Mind creates things and objects! While our father creates from faith! He provides everything in his time.

He is the awesome one of every act and play! I think he's the one who is in control of the motion picture now, watching the earth that he created, without a sound, he's all that! No one could defeat his purpose, because he's the time stopper of history! He's the game of each saying! He provides everything in his time. He is the awesome one of every act and play! I think he's the one who is in control of the motion picture now, watching the earth that he created, without a sound, he's all that! No one could defeat his purpose, because he's the time stopper of history! He's the game of each saying! He makes the call of everyone's awaken. The presence of his blessings is the gifts of life and the big, beautiful, bright stars and the moon! My love for you is like a never ending rain, full of stars above and the comet of Mars. Nothing can break the force of my love from revealing it's truth being as one, me and you, the full contact that it gives bringing forth love, peace, and harmony of care. I myself can't understand it, but that I do know my god has planned it! These are the days and times that I find my chosen beauty from the hidden rooted one of this reality. My heart will be as a maze searching for my beautiful Queen in this un forbidden consciousness stage of a higher learning.

The uniqueness of your personality will be the pathway for me being closer to you. Allowing yourself of yours take control of my eternity maze of troops. The time has come for every human being to get there selves together because god is sending signs that is very powerful and very believable for all human kind. At this time I don't know where life will take me, but I do know this much and that is god takes care of all his children. I lay down and dream about all sorts of things, to me life is a dream, a dream of believing into accomplishes anything in life that you possibly can. Your answers come from within your dreams, the dream of your natural reality. That forms your world of being that force of light. It's a very powerful thing to me that force gives me knowledge and also provides insight on society's challenges. Life is a very special thing to experience it has a lot of opportunities for all different sorts of cultures; it's beautiful, you feel so free and relaxed about life. As the glimpse of love takes over your mind and soul you begin to release your pain and frustration to come in contact with the creator! The only one! Full of love bliss, and love fulfilling every intimate part of you for his phenomenal needs. Blending things together in time for every woman and mans needs as of human beings. We are the ones that procrastinate and our lord is he who puts us back in line. There's no one as bodacious as he, because he's the resource, the omnipresent. Playing everybody's role in this illusion of uniqueness! So I say all things come together like a magnet! In his time as it is written we have to allow him to design our hearts and soul taking control of the motions for every man and woman! He's the creator of time passing his unique skills that's so fine into his creations of the mind! With no repercussions just love him and relax in the bliss of love! That would take your mind away from time. Lifestyles and challenges of destruction, corruption blowing your mind mixed up foolishness playing the game back and forth until your soul is doomed! I know that everything comes from god it's a beautiful unique feeling once it starts flowing through! It's unstoppable so pure and sweet it creates its form of energy from our father! It's somewhat like an interjecting feeling that is connected to a power but I know in my heart it's the feeling of love! God is the bliss of love! There is only one God, no images of God, there's only the creation of love! And it's so much your heart achieves from love combined with God's love! What do you have? Heal the heart. Treat the heart with love. Leave the heart in peace! Always stay alert of the heart because it's of love! Sometimes I ask myself why I was brought into this existence. The purpose was love! That's what this reality is about. That is how the creator feels the bliss, through his elements that he created. I pray for love and understanding from you because only the spirits in tune with your thoughts so therefore I base my heart on the force of love! I know love means more than hurting someone's feelings and also love plays an outstanding structure in our reality! Love is so pure and it cuts through the heart of God's creations. That's why through the uniqueness of love we will always have life from up above. The peace at night for everything that God created. I feel the quiet sounds that echoes in my heart.

The beats are continuous I try to understand the emotional tunes of peace, but there's always something that interferes with getting the full understanding of God's creation. I feel the peace that the father granted me, and it's of love no one can't steal from me, because my father instilled in my heart! With his songs of melody, and harmony, He gave me a talent to use not throwaway, but to have faith and continue on! The peace will continue to flow from my father's will. I write what I see and feel, my love within creates my life of being. There's so much that I would like the unseen to see what is within me, but my life isn't to be destined here, and I know I won't learn anything in the nick of time. I do know this much that my beloved spirit has opened up to me. I am learning more about it each and every day, but if it wasn't for my heavenly father I wouldn't know anything but how to be a wannabe or a lost soul! I feel peace, love, and harmony within my heart. It takes over my being inherited at birth. It performs the holiness of glow! Spreading love is like a touch of devotion, putting yourself into deep conversation, letting your feelings of emotion play the part of spreading love full of deep emotion. Spreading love can cause heartache to those that always continue to cause much hate, blocking them from receiving the gift of spreading love. Spreading love can make you or break you receiving that joy that will uplift you and caress your soul. That's why this gift is called spreading love! Walking through the dimensions of your mind and speaking to someone dark and blind . . . . Not knowing before time your image pictured in the mind already designed for you to make it through these days and times . . . . I am a young African king, a brother that was put here on this plantation to serve my father's creation. Sacrificing my life to obtain my faith in fulfilled grace. God is so unique he gives us the talent to express how he feels about his children. We function through grace of his forgiveness. He is the source of our forgiveness. He knows every step before we make it! He is so pure nothing can stop him. When released the sounds of earth are the secrets to the living!

Love is beautiful, it overcomes every trail in your life style, and it is the boldness of your talk and the swiftness of your heart and the most of all the pureness of your appearance. To become this love you must submit yourself to the pureness up above, so beautiful, fine, and divine, to be in design for his children below this fragile time. Love brings you up and sometimes breaks you down, but when you have someone from above, a higher power with the forgiveness of open arms to lift you up from your nightmare of the devil's souls. The serenity of love is a very unique creation of life, because there's nothing but love in the eyes of that creature. Life is a journey for every man's heart creating time now for everyone's part. To play the game of life, where so many of us depart into an unknown place we called space, looking for the portion of the makeover we call clay, scientific chemistry of the body input is mysterious maze for humans to come and realize that is of the body, itself, and now that's it's energy became so strong and powerful until it's beautiful feeling is so full of bliss, that it cannot be explained, but I only try to understand it, myself because they are my thoughts, slipping and sliding through time is not mine. There's so much to do in this lifetime with the love of the sprinkling of seeds across God's reality, full of joy and pleasure for this lost society, as I speak from within, the sounds of my thoughts begun to blend, and my heart speaks of strokes of tunes that continue on with my love blooming, if only I could just feel the unseen of myself with a touch of love. I cry each and everyday, bleeding from my heart toward a touch of love. Love is bliss of a foundation because once you feel it, it separates you from this reality, and it is awesome how it takes control of you. It is unique that God's creation of joy is a blessing just to get a touch that makes me feel so strong from the rest of the world. I feel so good down inside to be able to let this pride free it itself from the pureness of love. I know that my lord is watching over me.

The sound of love is in the music from up above, it reveal its beauty and emotional feeling out towards those who don't have pride in their hearts, its beautiful because the love that flows out of gospel music and beautiful melody that is apart of you, because music is beautiful and it plays and exercises your truth, especially the kind that takes control of your heart, filled with so much intents until its so uncontrolled, only the soul of your heart can feed off that beat of your soul. Love is the true blue, to be real, so to say; my heart provides plenty of it to you, bringing forth everlasting love such as two white beautiful godly doves, seeking the beauty with each other's soul. I just wish that you could feel what I become to accept to feel but in time, the truthfulness of destiny will reveal the meaning of love, the sweetness of love is so smooth, it performs a touch of beauty, generating from the heart of doves, so unique that nothing can break the pureness of the shadow touch as it flows through the system of many individual gushing out like a fountain of purity so real, and rich feeling with the lord' blessings of peace on its covering top on individuals, design is so unique that it brings forth love and discipline to each one of us that our heavenly father's stepping stone brings forth the knowledge of love, showing his care from up above. We are his creatures.

# Chapter 9

## Peace

Everybody's destiny has been ordained since birth, we're all alike in this so called reality that has so much excitement in it, and it's created to be the worst. Young brothers and sisters are constantly dying day by day, but if they could only see their truthfulness, there would be no wars amongst God's creation and time, killing one another for what the other one had to struggle for, not knowing it's you my brother, killing off yourselves and each other. Take time to think about the Evil doer, it's not you it's the evil brother; we have been brainwashed to think that as you. I must say the spirit is what we are and what God conformed us to be. Beauty, amongst generations proud and with dignity, I stretch out my arms openly, to my brothers and sisters, hoping that we can teach one another, bring forth the seed of sweetness and true color, throughout this world. May our love be expressed in so many ways, God you, so stop the stress and 'killing one another my brothers and sisters.

Everyone is always downing their own kind, God created us equally to love, share, and come together as one, he gave us one thought of his portion to come to the understanding of his gift, he gave us one talent, that so many of us loving doing and everything he gave us was as one, just as himself as I am. If you notice, everyone hasn't done anything different from the other creature on this earth, everything is the same, and it is just explained in many different ways of aspect. I am a gift to many of my brothers and sisters for those that don't know my father, but want to know him, for the heart is the kingdom of heaven, where my father built his many mansions from the foundation of the earth, the temple of peace and meekness. The thoughts of master minded people increased the knowledge that God implied about his creatures with the ability to create the reality with beauty and to fulfill things, not the corruption that the world destroys human beings with, as reality plays it's role to breathe, it's nature's code is exhaling the dead and the living, each and everyday, as we live, we get an answer from God for the new awakening for better awareness and letting the spirit be in stillness with the creator that his heavenly bliss for God's children with open arms, he loves us a zillion times, more than you think. He gave his only begotten son, to this lifelong world to change the hearts of sinners that are lost in this description of criminalizing the mind with baggage until there's no escape from the fear of your soul.

The thoughtless and faultless times that we are living in, there's so many of us pretending, hiding our true identity for falsehood serenity. God knows his spirits of love, he controls the love and lost souls, he gives and he takes away, because he's the completeness of this weakness, this so called reality. God has given each individual a grace of love, but so many of us lose that spiritual flow, it's the life of this reality, we are just living this life for those who fought the battle of freedom and for those who gave up bleeding for us, and didn't fight without uniting as one with the truthfulness of being secluded, creating your abode, a bliss with the heavenly form of creation, testing the realization from no land of direction from the streets above your intersection. Visions are hidden from every man seeking acceptance of the challenges we go through, beyond this earth, full of fruit that no human can take.

How can thoughts change the time? I don't have a clue, but maybe I'll just sit back and enjoy the view seeking to increase the knowledge of the option to experience hitting to incline my mind, pushing a zillion wart balls into my spiritual plan, specializing, contrastalizing my life experiences beyond the factual place of reality, beautiful stars, above the firm and trees of faith and harmony. The ocean is like a shallow bliss of smooth silk, filled with pleasure to feel your needs to ease away your pain when attempt is near. Pretty soon the raft will end the days of a new life will begin in the eyes of the lord, the world will proclaim the strength of the new beginners! Pretty soon things will be in time of destruction of a platoon, a virus that won't end, killing off the sinful and much more, pretending to be the hell raiser of the world!!

The eyes of the doves are filled with so much uniqueness of love, so truly expressed until there's none above this beautiful love. The quality that we give here on earth is for our father to obtain us and train us into a new creature at birth, love is everywhere, but do we know this love? It is full of so much inner suspense, heavenly creations by our father, free of charge for every human of God's creation, everybody has this macho type reality filled with so much brutality, until they become blind of this world's society. Common lifestyles that are rich and famous about every little thing that goes on in life, always repeats itself around the surface again and again, truly life is a very unset sight seeing for the most of us, the rejecting times of life's experiences so very confusing from childhood's reality. The mind of the thoughts are void and stillness is so peaceful to seek knowledge from within until the brain is animated and manipulated, bringing the consciousness alive, fully in control of everything so unique and brilliant until it becomes life's instrument of reality, the time of everything, human's creative actions are a gift from God, not to say before the mind could not accept anything from reality.

Peace is at a higher level, it doesn't measure up to the length of this reality, it is freely born, no escape from it, it's a gift from the lord. Peace overcomes these lifestyles of this reality; there are so many things that get in the way of your peace that you can't let it get the best of your joy, because peace is a blossom of your ability to increase your discipline and knowledge. Your dreams are your deep reality that goes beyond this outside appearance of stage challenges so far until God can see your spirit in man. Dreams are invisible to the flesh, only the unseen can visualize the glow of the pureness of the spirit of man. God is like a picture in so many ways, full of so many dreams in a very unique way that the stronger we become in contact with power, no one can destroy our uplifting desires.

The time is coming when everybody should know their secluded one, the one who appears in the vision of every human being with the bliss of love and peace, the rhythm of your thoughts are full of a foundation from God of love, so sweet and beautiful, that people can't understand how strong the wisdom comes to be the flow of love within the healing of songs, exploring life's destiny is like a maze puzzle, full of uncontrolled situations, life is so confused until there's no way out of your mind zone. We are dimensions of our minds, we create good or bad in our life, we create heaven or hell, the mind is like the key to heaven, but the heart takes the place of love and love is everything of birth, the mind is set for time, but the heart is designed for peace, joy, and forgiveness for most charities, mind, thoughts, creation, reality, existence of being, time . . . time . . . . time . . . , through the inner man of eternity. There are so many perseverates, people in this world today living their own phenomenal lives as philosophers, when the creator who created everybody as one, trying to be the God of their own, knowing that the secluded one is the savior of everybody's home, the secret place that is in the heart, but humans don't realize the beauty of love and forgiveness in the eyes of their enemies.

There is something in me that I call the spirit of man, it has no appearance, it creates life just like trees create fruit and the land of this reality is an illusion of vision theory. Everything is developed from faith and everything lives on by faith that is how love created us, through bliss of total faith, when love created this reality, it created every possible form of every beast that could possibly fit the form of reality. The essence of my life is absolutely revealing in the eyes of the lord with sincere presence of his life to his creatures from within, out towards reality, sharing his love through the hearts, spiritual souls for the sake of his creation abode, blissfully it cuts through the flesh like a sword, so pure and filled with the cure of wisdom and everlasting lifetime of freedom. The thundering of the beat and harmony, the vocals of the strong strokes, forcing the bolts of power out of this beautiful instrument of the heart that the lord created, spreading out the musical beat of love for his creation, knocking the sinners down with the blows of pureness, bass thumping on the heart with the pumping tunes out of the mouth, it comes searching for the lost souls.

# Chapter 10

## Stress

God gives me hope even through the work, the pain bleeds through the veins. It's so hard being a black man, even as I lay down to shut my eyes and close my ears, my mind remains aware of the deep thoughts, so far and deep into a spiritual rim, obtained in my father's book of creation for the sake of everyone's existence, standing high like the uniqueness of his one hundred percent creation, we weren't meant to be misled until materialistic things came into this reality, searching for the sign of love, lost in this disruptional place of drugs, corrupting everyone's mind with the types of scams and plans, fooling you and tricking you from the freedom of God's plan.

The struggles that people go through in life are so cruel and destine that we as creatures go through, the suffering will cross every woman's and man's oath that is sufficient, there will be joy and laughter, but the pain will always be there for the test of life's challenges. The dreams of every human are within themselves to discover and find to win the history of human minds, to leave a legacy behind for all kind, the future of the new born birth will be designed for all people. I think and wonder each and every day about my brothers and sisters, I think about stuff that is so confusing for some people, I know that I have a mind of my own, but there's so many things that people try to throw at me with their thoughts, but God makes me recognize the things he knows the love of his spirit. I am just a human being here in this world of today, expressing myself through the spirit and soul that the lord gave me with beautiful eyes to see, a mouth to taste, and a nose to smell with ears to listen with, hands to feel and arms to lift, feet to walk with, legs to stand on, the lord did all these things in his time to design his unity as one, connecting all parts of the body, time will go on when I'm dead and gone in remembrance, I'll leave the truth behind for all mankind.

The thoughts and looks of a black man plays his character and appearance based on this reality, a black man has needs for his selfish deeds, we are always into something that doesn't belong to us, we always want to be the star of each awakening show, we have the talents to achieve every kind deed, but so many of us lose focus of our potentials and securities of spiritual deeds, as a black man, we were put here for a purpose to see the side of outer limits of our appearance. We are the eyes of this reality in getting the respect that we deserve from the beginning of life. The blacks are always downing one another when we should be speaking the truth of our forefathers; the killer instinct of a black man never dies until that person returns back into dirt and mold. The story and legacy a black man leaves behind always puts the younger one in tune with his kind because the honor of a black man speaks out for the justice that they stood up for, fighting for the lost souls of this reality, the black man would always be in the existence of reality, speaking for myself, we need to let go of our pride and come together with and dignity. But the love of God reveals all things in the sight of human's access. It's only a matter of time that we all will have to depart from this stage, so those in this lifetime including every kind of person has a price to pay, to honor and glorify God.

The coolness we have in our everyday thoughts, the emotional groove we struck our hips to, feeling so good, enjoying our nature of reality being the peaceful, royal kings on earth with all respect to our queens first, sharing our most deepest weaknesses of inner thoughts towards them, being a philosopher in our time, seducing them with the notorious beauty of our unique tongue with so much romance of divinity, just you and her playing the role of love, feeling so good, you can feel the desire and how bad she wants it, licking her from her neck, up to her ears, she's saying, "STOP BABY, IT FEELS SO GOOD, PLEASE STOP". So you take it to another level, the player that you are, kissing her so well, while her slow song is playing, dancing in the moonlight, undressed from head to toe, getting so hot until there's no more desire left and you know the rest. Those brothers that don't have an African queen are lost in the sauce of the "Wanna Be's". Life is form of pain and destruction that starts from this reality of materialistic wants and not things that we need, destroying the inner seeds, the love of every individual provides the assumption of producing it's own energy and fear, sustaining the format of God's career, pleading to the blood of Jesus Christ with the fear every morning, I feel that burst of faith, fulfilling my father's grace, that gives me the way to keep believing that there are new beginnings in overcoming myself of fleshly wealth. Men and women will see the light when the darkest hour strikes, the sight of the just and the unjust for it's is forbidden for the corruption and shedding blood amongst the love that is in you, I am the spirit that my father created to be as a plan, forming the ways of reality from a distance standing, looking for a solution to push up upon my father's plan. Corrupting, criticizing, and vandalizing the force of evil economics features the production of civilization unjustly of false creations, trapped in this brutalization of an organized plan, neglecting the ones who made the time in his mind, not knowing he is life within his self, producing all those things from within, out towards reality, when we are the ones that turned it around and used it as brutality. The chemistry of the bodies of males and females produced us to become spiritually awakened, not knowing before time took birth into reality, the creator spoke of this unknown world into existence with the dreams of every unborn spirit filled with joy by creating the minds of human technology, so powerful, like computers, but we don't live off of computers, we live off of knowledge, you see, God is our provider to keep our chips running and we are connected to his energy, our eyes are like photos in a camera and the mind is like a movie script, never forgetting the times of our lives. But how can you live in harmony when the evil doer instruct us with materialistic deeds, instead of the secret needs.

The changing of history is caught up in the wickedness, transforming their minds to be the killer of each minority race, the changing of history is done to mankind by creating his time as he created time, every man should bow down to the most secluded, designated form from within this reality. So never try to play the world in your hands because you are going to lose the game! The misconception, disruptional, intellectual, brutalizing, utilizing, analyzing, disfunctionalizing, and scandalizing technology on human's ability with the control of the government, beating up yourself for something that's temporary for the eyes of many, but to sell and make money is plenty, no one on this earth will take the price of temporary things with them when they depart, their appearance of the inner soul, so the government will trick the ego and pride; that is everyone's downfall for those who fall short of the glory for the lord's book of storytelling.

I am really trying to figure out who I am. Is this really me playing this form of life? Or am I just repeating someone else's lifetime? I really don't know but I sit back and I think about so much stuff, it's like a dream that is so powerful, the dream of me, someone who doesn't even exist for real, but yet I have this connection to all materialistic substantial needs. I am very scared of this now and I think I am here but I don't have a clue about what I must do, to answer to the father-the omniscient, but in my words and thoughts, I would like to help my brothers and sisters before I return to the creator. The provocative ideas that we speak with thoughts that the mind creates and not from the heart is because the mind is so confused and mixed up in this illusion with the materialistic needs, not acknowledging their deeds for being here on this earth, specializing their minds to become their own enemies of many human beings, just as they are utilizing their kind for nothing, killing innocent people because of the power and higher authority for the next fool or president's story or must I speak the words of honor and glory.

Everybody wants to be a king and queen in this dream of reality, not knowing that everyone has to die and go home to the true reality, the reality of God's house but for right now, we are all living in a dream of make believe. The inner exceptional, egotistical, positive, and negative thoughts of the mind that God created for a tool that destroys the temple of the inner being without giving it time to manifest it's truthfulness of this reality, destroying it's inner source of the creational, talented things interfering with the power that your creator created, which is you from a speck of dust. Everybody has a different concept of attitude about everything, all sorts of challenges and experiences going on in this world. So many of God's children are dying with diseases, I wish that everything could be so good but I know if everything was good, we wouldn't have to go through life without a struggle without knowing God, that is why he's able to forgive us because he knows us, loves us, and sin is the mixture of our flesh, so therefore forgiveness is everlasting for us. Everybody wants to have a belief in something but don't want to sacrifice everything for their belief!

I believe that a belief is knowing that God is your protector and also he is searching to know your true self, the very truthfulness of you is an unlimited infinity that is everlasting, so therefore when you learn how to deal with the power, you will overcome a lot of negative things and also you will be able to come to know yourself of love, the full bliss of love. People are clowns of themselves, the game has been played so many times from another human being until everyone accepted the game line, now that's how wanna be's come in the picture, following the next man's decision, fooling themselves with the game of death, trying to be slick when there's no tricks for the stupidity that you perform from a empty thought in the trigger of your mind zone. So many are lost, the brothers are laughing in your face but all the time they are trying to steal your soul, that God gave you, there's nowhere to hide, there's no one that you can trust, but the lord knows the ones that you think that are okay, not because they are with the game of keeps themselves, I know only my spirit can separate me from those who are playing the enemy role of wanna be's.

Act as you speak, not to teach and pretend to be the black man that would catch one of your brother's attention, leading them in the right way of ascending. We are all supposed to be equal but God said, let there be peace and love for those that love him and believe in him. There's no peace or love in the hearts of the evil doer. Thoughts are an illusion, created from a form of nothing, designed to be something in the eyes of every human being, the thought can be good or bad, the thought is somewhat like birth, but different because of the seed formed with different realities, the thought is expressing and the birth was created of human beings, one's thoughts are a form of expression, forever and will live on throughout this concept of reality. Thoughts are so unique and re playing childish games, there comes a time in everyone's life when he or she must take on their own responsibility to live and with the help of beautiful, kind people like you and the support of my family, I think I'll make it, if it's God's will. The suffering of every kind is blind along with negativity, no one suffers, only the mind pretends to beat up the thoughts for reasonable structure of appearance, the mind plays on the ego for simple fault and once you become aware of yourself, you can adapt to something that doesn't matter, for real, because nothing can hurt you in this reality but you, if you let the word of someone affect you, it's because you allowed your ego accept that thought. The mind is always infuriated with the words of thoughts, it's easy to mislead the mind, to do negative things, the ego stirs up trouble for those that are losers and don't think that they have a struggle, for they are the ones that will repeat the doom of reality's challenges.

# Chapter 11

## The Ways of Mankind

The ways of mankind, killing our brothers with the 9 is leading us in the blind, the ways of mankind, killing our brothers with the 9, wake up and use your mind.

We as people should come together in peace and harmony and leave all of the violence behind.

Last night, when I was watching the news, a young brother shot a child, he was a juvenile, so much of life as a kid, he got caught up in the fast lane and sold his life to the game, and now he's doing a 20 year bid for the crime that he did, the judge split his wig.

### Chorus

As I walk through the valley of the shadow of death, so many homies of mine don't know that they're truly blessed, able to wake up each morning and pat their son on the shoulder and thank the lord up above for his unconditional love, increasing knowledge that God implies, why is the black race so blind, we're only killing our own kind, wake it's pure genocide, we bleed all the same blood, will someone come an d show me some love and stop selling your brother dubs and show him some love.

First, the enemy, full of hope and envy, you aren't no friend to me, so don't pretend to be. God designed this world for us to live in together and to love each other, not to kill a brother, we were taught to hate our own kind and to lead them into the blindness of self destruction, now is the time to resurrect the mind of the deaf, dumb, and blind, now it's our time, we must stick together in stormy weather, the devil is clever, but he destroys us, OH never, it's birth that God gives and creates, so wake up brothers, THERE'S NO ESCAPE!